# Synthesis Lectures on Human-Centered Informatics

Editor
**John M. Carroll,** *Penn State University*

Human-Centered Informatics (HCI) is the intersection of the cultural, the social, the cognitive, and the aesthetic with computing and information technology. It encompasses a huge range of issues, theories, technologies, designs, tools, environments and human experiences in knowledge work, recreation and leisure activity, teaching and learning, and the potpourri of everyday life. The series will publish state-of-the-art syntheses, case studies, and tutorials in key areas. It will share the focus of leading international conferences in HCI.

Making Claims: Knowledge Design, Capture, and Sharing in HCI
D. Scott McCrickard
2012

HCI Theory: Classical, Modern, and Contemporary
Yvonne Rogers
2012

Activity Theory in HCI: Fundamentals and Reflections
Victor Kaptelinin and Bonnie Nardi
2012

Conceptual Models: Core to Good Design
Jeff Johnson and Austin Henderson
2011

Geographical Design: Spatial Cognition and Geographical Information Science
Stephen C. Hirtle
2011

User-Centered Agile Methods
Hugh Beyer
2010

# Making Claims
### Knowledge Design, Capture, and Sharing in HCI

Making Claims: Knowledge Design, Capture, and Sharing in HCI

D. Scott McCrickard

ISBN: 978-3-031-01070-5    paperback
ISBN: 978-3-031-02198-5    ebook

DOI 10.1007/978-3-031-02198-5

A Publication in the Springer series
*SYNTHESIS LECTURES ON HUMAN-CENTERED INFORMATICS*

Lecture #15
Series Editor: John M. Carroll, *Penn State University*
Series ISSN
Synthesis Lectures on Human-Centered Informatics
Print 1946-7680    Electronic 1946-7699

# Making Claims

## Knowledge Design, Capture, and Sharing in HCI

D. Scott McCrickard
Virginia Tech

*SYNTHESIS LECTURES ON HUMAN-CENTERED INFORMATICS #15*

# ABSTRACT

Human-centered informatics (HCI) is a young discipline that is still defining its core components, with approaches rooted in engineering, science, and creative design. In the spirit of this book series, this book explores HCI as an intersection point for different perspectives of computing and information technology, seeking to understand how groups of designers can communicate with an increasingly diverse set of colleagues on a broadening set of problems. In so doing, this book traces the evolution of claims as a way to capture and share knowledge, particularly in comparison to other approaches like patterns and issues. Claims can be a centrally important aspect in HCI design efforts, either consciously by targeted design techniques or through ingrained habits of experienced designers. An examination of claims, their uses in design, and the possibilities for explicit use in future collaborative design endeavors seeks to inspire their further development use in HCI design.

# KEYWORDS

claims, patterns, issues, IBIS, knowledge capture, usability engineering, creative design, design rationale, reuse

# Contents

# Preface

This book is about making claims: the development of knowledge in collaborative situations by groups of people with differing skills and opinions. Claims appeal to me because they are simple in many ways, but they hide a rich complexity that can be leveraged to drive design from the perspectives of engineering, science, or creativity. I try to reflect the simplicity of claims early in the book, then reveal the complexities (and the possibilities) for claims as a knowledge capture and sharing mechanism as the book evolves. Claims are not the only knowledge capture method for HCI: I set out to bring together three core methods—claims, issues, and patterns—to trace their evolution and to consider how they can contribute to the design of interactive systems.

This book is a monograph, part of a series on Human Centered Informatics (HCI), a young field still seeking to define itself. The primary audience is people in academia—those interested in the evolution of the ideas related to knowledge capture in HCI. That said, I feel that Chapters 1 and 5 are both highly accessible for any audience. Chapters 2 and 3 provide a high-level view of early advances in knowledge capture that helped define the way we know things in HCI. Chapter 4 provides an in-depth view of how claims have been used in some research and development projects in academia and industry; this chapter may be of interest to those who want to view the methods in action. Finally, in the spirit of this book, Appendix A positions a series of 20 claims about claims (and patterns and issues) in a timeline view that is easily browsable.

Given the flux in the field of HCI, it may seem like an odd time to write a book that talks about the ways to capture something so dynamic. My thought is that there is no perfect time to write a book, but there is no bad time either. This book represents my current view on things, but even (perhaps especially) in the course of writing this book my views have changed. I welcome comments about omissions, corrections, and new directions—it will go into one of the next things I write! (And I hope you will help me with it.)

Parts of this book have been based on material from prior papers that I had a hand in authoring, in particular Chapter 4. All of these papers include co-authors who often had a greater role than I in writing the papers—I'm very grateful for the chance to work with such an inspirational and hard-working group of people. Specifically, the opening of Chapter 4 draws from a 2004 ACM SIGCSE paper on teaching HCI with engineering, science, and design methods [McCrickard et al., 2004]. The cases throughout the rest of Chapter 4 are adapted from the following papers: Section 4.1.1 from a DIS paper [Chewar et al., 2004b]; Section 4.1.2 from an Agile paper [Lee et al., 2008] and a CHI case study [Lee et al., 2011]; Section 4.2.1 from a CHI note [Bhatia and McCrickard, 2006]; Section 4.2.2 from an ACHI paper [Karam et al., 2009]; and Section 4.3.2 from a paper in the

Human Technology Journal [McCrickard et al., 2011], which built on a series of papers at IFIP Interact, DIS, and CHI [Wahid et al., 2009, 2010, 2011].

D. Scott McCrickard
May 2012

# Acknowledgments

I am fortunate to have worked with four excellent Ph.D. students, who really pulled me along with their great ideas and tremendous enthusiasm: Christa Chewar, Jacob Somervell, Jason Chong Lee, and Shahtab Wahid. Next up is Ph.D. candidate Jeremy Barksdale, who has been making great progress with limited interactions with me. I am grateful to my other students and collaborators on projects related to this book: Miten Sampat, Stacy Branham, Jan Willem Streefkerk, Maria Karam, Cyril Montabert, Jamie Smith, Brandon Berry, Chris Allgood, Chuck Holbrook, Ali Ndiwalana, Saurabh Bhatia, Todd Stevens, Tejinder Judge, Laurian Vega, Lauren Cairco, Joe DeGol, and Nina Elias. I suspect all of these people can find their words and ideas in this book!

This book would not have come together had it not been for collaborations with Steve Harrison, Alistair Sutcliffe, John M. Carroll, Mary Beth Rosson, Alex Zhao, and John Stasko. The Human Computer Interaction Consortium (HCIC) meetings have been extremely inspirational; of particular benefit was the HCIC 2009 "Theory in HCI" panel that I organized with Scott Klemmer that featured Stu Card, Clayton Lewis, Deborah Tatar, and Jim Hollan.

I am grateful to Virginia Tech and the University of Colorado, Boulder for supporting my sabbatical in 2011–2012, both financially and logistically. Thanks also to the NSF (IIS-1135149) for their financial support. Over the years, funding from NSF, NIST, the Virginia Tech ASPIRES program, Google, and Microsoft has supported the background efforts that led to this book.

I appreciate the great academic atmosphere at the University of Colorado, Boulder; the long discussions about the book with Ray McCall and Clayton Lewis, and engaging conversations about HCI directions with Leysia Palen, Ken Anderson, Gerhard Fischer, and Katie Siek. It would have been difficult to complete this book without the intellectual stimulation from my sabbatical time here. Also emerging from my sabbatical are future theoretical efforts in claims, design, usability engineering, and knowledge capture, as well as applied projects related to cognitive disabilities and limitations. I also appreciate electronic exchanges with Kailash Awati, Paul Clumsee, Al Selvin, Simon Buckingham Shum, Michelle Bachler, Janet Burge, and John Thomas. I'm thankful for the time all of these people (and many others) spent commenting on early thoughts and responding to odd email queries…it's tough when the whole world isn't on sabbatical with me!

I am grateful for the guidance of the series editor, John M. Carroll, and to Diane Cerra from Morgan & Claypool, for the opportunity to write this book and for their encouragement during the process. I appreciate the rapid and detailed reviews of an early version of this book from John Thomas, Ray McCall, Clayton Lewis, John M. Carroll, Jason Chong Lee, and Shahtab Wahid—they gave me a great many suggestions, and following them all will keep me busy for a very long time.

Finally, I appreciate the support from my wife, Lisa Wenner McCrickard, and our three children, Gordon, Grady, and Gwen. May the adventures continue!


D. Scott McCrickard
May 2012

# Figure Credits

**Figure** 4.1    McCrickard, D. S., Chewar, C. M., Somervell, J. P., and Ndiwalana, A. 2004. A model for notification systems evaluation—Assessing user goals for multitasking activity. ACM Transactions on Computer-Human Interaction (TOCHI) 10 (4), 312-338. Montreal, Quebec, Canada: ACM. Copyright ©2003, ACM. Used with permission. DOI: 10.1145/966930.966933

**Figure** 4.2    Lee, J. C., McCrickard, D. S., and Stevens, K. T. 2008. Examining the Foundations of Agile Usability with eXtreme Scenario-Based Design. In Proceedings of the 2009 Conference on Agile Software Development (Agile 2009), 3-10. Copyright ©2009 IEEE. Used with permission. DOI: 10.1109/AGILE.2009.30

**Figure** 4.3    Karam, M., Lee, J. C., Rose, T., Quek, F., McCrickard, D. S. 2009. Comparing gesture and touch for notification system interaction. In Proceedings of the 2009 IARIA Conference on Advances in Computer Human Interaction (ACHI), 7-12. Copyright ©2009 IEEE. Used with permission. DOI: 10.1109/ACHI.2009.65

**Figure** 4.4    Wahid, S. S. 2011. *Facilitating design knowledge reuse through relationships.* Ph.D. dissertation, Department of Computer Science, Virginia Tech. Used with permission.

**Figure** 4.5    McCrickard, D. S., Wahid, S., Branham, S. M., and Harrison, S. 2011. Achieving Both Creativity and Rationale: Reuse in Design with Images and Claims. Human Technology 7 (2), 109-122. ©2011 Agora Center, University of Jyväskylä. Used with permission.

**Figure page** 77    Begeman, M. L. and Conklin, J. 1988. The right tool for the job. Byte Magazine. 255-266. Used with permission.

**Figure page** 79    illustration courtesy of Ray McCall.

**Figure page** 84    Selvin, A. 1999. Supporting collaborative analysis and design with hypertext functionality. *Journal of Digital Information 1* (4). ©1999 Texas Digital Library. Used with permission.

**Figure page 86**   van Duyne, D. K., Landay, J. A., and Hong, J. I. 2006. *The Design of Sites: Patterns for Creating Winning Web Sites, Second Edition.* Copyright ©2007, Pearson Education, Inc., Prentice Hall. Used with permission.

**Figure page 89**   Saponas, T. S., Prabaker, M. K., Abowd, G. D., and Landay, J. A. 2006. The impact of pre-patterns on the design of digital home applications. Eds. Proceedings of the 2006 international conference on Designing Interactive Systems. pp. 189-198. Montreal, Quebec, Canada: ACM. Copyright ©2006, ACM. Used with permission. DOI: 10.1145/1142405.1142436

**Figure page 91**   Zahler, T. 2010. *A Usability Engineering Lifecycle for Applications in Safety-Related Environments.* Ph.D. dissertation, University of Technology Vienna. Used with permission.

**Figure page 92**   Wahid, S. S. 2011. *Facilitating design knowledge reuse through relationships.* Ph.D. dissertation, Department of Computer Science, Virginia Tech. Used with permission.

**Figure page 93**   Awati, K. 2011. Capturing decision rationale on projects. Eight to late. http://eight2late.wordpress.com/2011/03/10/capturing-decision-rationale-on-projects/. Used with permission.

# CHAPTER 1

# What are Claims?

## AN INVESTIGATION OF THE ORIGINS

Claims capture knowledge in a way that can be shared, debated, strengthened, rebutted, connected, and reused. The modern colloquial notion of claims stems from Stephen Toulmin's use of the term in his classic 1958 book, *The Uses of Argument*, in which he positions claims as a falsifiable proposition meant to be supported or refuted with data. Claims were introduced to the field of human-computer interaction (HCI) in the late 1980s, at a time when researchers and practitioners were looking for ways to engage theory, exchange information, and cross boundaries toward common design goals. But the changing landscape of the discipline has resulted in new problems, and new ways of approaching problems—centered more on the human than the technology—requiring that we look again at how claims can be part of the landscape of our discipline.

This book traces the evolution of claims, particularly with respect to other approaches to knowledge capture, design reuse, and design rationale. This book argues for claims as a centrally important aspect in the creation of HCI—one that often becomes integrated in successful design efforts, either consciously or through the habits of experienced designers. It is my hope that a pointed look at the evolution of claims, their uses in design, and the possibilities for explicit use in future collaborative design endeavors will encourage close consideration for their use by novice and experienced designers.

## 1.1   MOTIVATION

There is a need in HCI for unifying approaches that can draw together the diverse research fields that contribute to the discipline. In particular, this book considers ways that HCI knowledge is captured and shared—reflecting upon the evolution of approaches with respect to the changing nature of HCI as a discipline. Exploring these themes highlights the balance between freedom and boundedness in HCI: a need to break rules that do not seem to apply to our changing discipline, and a need to create rules that help further our endeavors. This work explores ways to undertake HCI knowledge capture and sharing, even (especially!) as our discipline continues to define itself.

To explain why I chose to focus on claims, it is important to reflect upon the nature of the discipline of HCI—indeed, what it is that will make HCI a coherent and long-lasting discipline. Long and Dowell [1989] note that key characteristics of a *discipline* include knowledge, practice, and a general problem. Their definitions for those terms with respect to the current state of HCI were very broad in their scope, with proposed solutions so broad that many of the creators of such comprehensive methods agreed overstepped any overarching expectations [Carroll, 2010; Diaper,

2002]. However, there is some agreement that the focus on knowledge, practice, and problem provides a reasonable framework for defining a discipline [Carroll, 2010; Sutcliffe, 2002].

Probing HCI within this framework, I would argue that HCI has not yet reached the stage where it can be considered a discipline—there is little agreement regarding what makes up important knowledge, accepted practice, or even core problems for HCI. Each subdiscipline has its own knowledge, practice, and problems that are considered important, and the largest conference in the area, ACM SIGCHI, evaluates submissions by assigning them to topical committees (e.g., engineering, user experience, digital arts) that have a large amount of autonomy in accepting papers—removing any need for agreement across the committees regarding importance of problem, validity of practice, or impactfulness of knowledge.

I don't mean this lack of agreement as an entirely bad thing for the short term: HCI is a young discipline that is still seeking to define itself, and we are fortunate that it has shifted in its focus, as participants in the area embrace and discard ideas toward developing their own field. This was reflected in the names for the field, as the term *man-machine interaction* from the 1970s gave way to terms like *computer-human interaction*, *human-computer interaction*, and *human-computer interfaces* adopted in the 1980s to reflect a focus on humans and computers as distinct and important entities whose interaction was worthy of intellectual attention. The fields of cognitive science, cognitive engineering, and psychology provided a basis for formal experimental and engineering processes that drove much of the early research in the field. Recent years have seen a shift in the field, and an accompanying shift in the terminology used to describe the field, to focus first on people and their needs for information and computing power—with emerging terms like *human-centered computing*, *human-centric computing*, and this book series' *human centered informatics*. This shift puts more focus on humans—not only on their interactions with technology, but on their own satisfaction, happiness, societal impact, and interaction with each other—drawing from fields that include sociology, architecture, and creative design. A great many excellent historical reflections delve into the early evolution of HCI (e.g., Carroll, 2010; Grudin, 2005).

Many authors seek to formally expand the problem space addressed by HCI by showing how new areas fit into the emerging discipline; as examples, Fallman [2003] describes different approaches to HCI design as conservative (engineering-based), pragmatic (science-based), or romantic (art-based); and Harrison et al. [2007] orders the sub-disciplines of HCI into three paradigms of engineering (including programming and ergonomics), science (laboratory, theoretical, and behavioral), and practice-based approaches (ethnography, action research, interaction analysis). By articulating these differences, the authors seek to highlight the different questions that can be asked in the HCI discipline, and the accompanying processes for addressing them. In addition, process-based approaches have been introduced that seek to introduce new methods to a community, (e.g., Gaver's [2000] cultural probes, designed to "provoke inspirational responses" rather than collect data for summary and analysis), or that seek to show how approaches can work together (e.g., van Setten et al.'s [1997]) Super Technique that diagrammed when and how to use existing interaction design techniques).

Rather than distinguish and emphasize the differences in approaches, this book seeks to show how they can be integrated—and to provide avenues to integrate other approaches, as they come up—toward a common foundation for HCI. Grudin [2005] notes that HCI has broken away from the foundational disciplines from which HCI originated—with promise of a new approach to HCI that might borrow from other approaches but is uniquely its own. This evolution of HCI seems unlikely to occur without tension, involving negotiation among researchers and practitioners from different backgrounds. This is exemplified in the two-part "Damaged Merchandise" special issue of IJHCS. The special issue was headlined by Gray and Salzman's journal article [1998a], in which the authors highlighted scientific inaccuracies in the methods used in five published experiments, each of which "had an important influence on HCI thought and practice". The special issue continued with rebuttals to the article by the authors of the five critiqued experiments [Olson and Moran, 1998], painting a picture of HCI as an emerging discipline that was defining its own set of methods—particularly for real-world situations that cannot be captured in lab settings. Gray and Salzman [1998b] concluded the special issue with a rejoinder, noting that definitions for key terms must be agreed upon for research to be useful to practitioners.

Many researchers and practitioners cast HCI as a "hybrid discipline" or "meta-discipline", integrating approaches from many disciplines without a well-defined identity of its own Carroll [2010]; Harrison et al. [2007]. But exchanges like the "Damaged Merchandise" one—and the changing nature of HCI conferences to include increasingly more meaningful rebuttal periods between authors and reviewers—suggests a desire for greater debate around the methods we use. We must not abandon approaches from the past, but we must be careful to make them our own, to consider how they fit with the changing needs of HCI. A term like *ethnography* is not used in HCI as they are in other disciplines (much to some people's great chagrin [Dourish, 2001] and a term like *usability* is an evolving construct with different meanings among researchers [Gray and Salzman, 1998b].

As the field continues to grow and as we train people with a broad view of HCI, I envision a community of people who identify not as cognitive engineers or psychologists, but first as HCI professionals—armed with methods adopted from a great many contributing branches of study but methods uniquely belonging to HCI. This new breed of professionals will have a broader sense of the HCI problem space and the processes to address the problems, but to be part of a meaningful discipline they will need a common knowledge base to capture and share their findings within the community.

This book explores approaches for knowledge capture and sharing in HCI, seeking to understand the key elements of a *lingua franca* for our discipline—a common language that is understood by all of the stakeholders in a design effort. This book certainly draws from these problem- and process-centric views of HCI, but its main focus is in the capture and sharing of knowledge. In that sense, it draws significantly from design rationale [Moran and Carroll, 1996], which captures the artifacts created in design with the reasoning behind the decisions for creating them. But it focuses specifically on the nature of the knowledge artifact—considering how it can be accepted in many HCI disciplines. Important in our exploration are Rittel's issues and Alexander's patterns, but we view Carroll's claims as a central point of study for this exploration—not only because of their history in argumentation and success with certain HCI problems, but also because of their potential moving forward.

## 1.2   DEFINITION

This section seeks to provide a definition for *claim* as it is used in the field of HCI. This is challenging because there have been many of definitions over the years. In some ways the entire book defines claims—how they compare to other approaches (Chapter 3), how they have been used (Chapter 4), and how they might evolve and be used in the future (Chapter 5). This section seeks to present a comprehensive definition for claims in HCI, rooted in a few key elements that are common to all uses of the term but seeking to include aspects that have been used to increase their utility.

As introduced broadly to the ACM SIGCHI community in Carroll and Kellogg [1989], two definitive features have been leveraged and expanded in every other use of the term in HCI: an artifact and its effects. Claim *artifacts* first referred to aspects of a user interface (like the size of a button or the amount of text on a screen) but has been used to refer to any feature of a situation regardless of its appearance or specifics about its behavior (such as "keyword search" or "placing a computer in a public space"). Claim *effects* in HCI describe what happens when the artifact is inserted into a situation, and generally are captured in terms of upsides (conveys information) and downsides (distracting) that reflect the tradeoffs of using the artifact. The effects initially focused on psychological effects—ways that the artifact would affect an individual who engaged with it—but shifted to describe any effect of the artifact on factors like computation speed, resource usage, or sociological effect. An example claim (adapted from McCrickard et al. [2003a]):

**Tickering text in the periphery of a desktop computer monitor:**

+ results in greater long-term knowledge gain of the displayed information than more static displays

− BUT leads to slower reaction times to changed information.

The artifact in the above claim is the text ticker, positioned on a desktop computer display. The upside (labeled with a "plus" sign) informs designers that users who have tickers on their desktops retain more knowledge of the information being animated across the screen compared to more static displays where the information is swapped a chunk at a time. The downside (labeled with a "minus" and starting with "BUT") reflects that users react more slowly using a ticker when they are tracking information for changes. A design team that encounters this claim would then have a starting point in deciding whether to use a ticker in their new design. (See A.5 for more on claims.)

Every claim in HCI captures these elements: the artifact and its effects (as upsides and downsides). While this is a fairly common format for a claim, a great many other formats have been used. In addition, claims often are much more complex than in this simple example, with additional knowledge to help designers make decisions about how to employ claims in their designs. More example claims are given in Appendix A; the remainder of this section introduces other common elements of claims.

There are other features that are commonly found in claims, many that were suggested in the original definition and formally elaborated in follow-up work. Most notably, in our simple example as in the original claims paper, the claim had only a single upside and a single downside—keeping it simple and focused, though arguably of limited use. In most uses, each claim can have multiple upsides and multiple downsides.

Claims typically lack context, and as such they tend to be associated with information that provides the context necessary to understand why the claim may be true. Most often, claims are associated with scenarios to provide this context [Carroll and Rosson, 1992]; indeed, they are presented as a secondary by-product of scenarios through scenario-based design (SBD) [Rosson and Carroll, 2002]. In the SBD approach, the scenario instantiates a concrete example of a problem, situation, or proposed solution, and one or more claims are identified and analyzed for each scenario. External to SBD, claims often have pointers or otherwise are associated with scenarios (and also sometimes to problems) to provide easy access to context for each claim [Sutcliffe, 2010; Sutcliffe and Carroll, 1999].

When claims are to be captured and stored for future access and reuse, additional features should be associated with them to assist in the browsing and search of claims libraries. Sutcliffe and Carroll [1999] call for many straightforward features that are suggested by prior work but never previously stated: a unique identifier, a title, an author list, and a natural language description of the claim. They also point out a need for a desired and measurable effect that should be produced by the claim, and complementing this, a list of dependencies required to realize the claim. Other work includes in the claim open design issues that can come up during the system implementation of the claim [Fabian et al., 2004].

Claims are falsifiable hypotheses—they are meant to spark discussion and study regarding their applicability for new situations. As such, researchers call for an explicit description of the motivating theory for the claim to be part of the claim [Sutcliffe, 2006; Sutcliffe and Carroll, 1999]. Others call for links to professional documents (e.g., usability studies or conference papers) from which a claim was derived [Wahid et al., 2010]. This type of knowledge gives designers the opportunity to make an informed judgement regarding their belief that a claim is valid for the design situation under consideration. For example, a claim based on a theory only valid for expert users (e.g., GOMS) should be questioned if the target user population is novices; and a claim based on a usability study with college-age participants might call for further investigation if the system under design is for seniors in an assisted living community.

Claims in isolation have limited use; it is when they are considered as a collection, or *library*, that it becomes possible to compare them—toward choosing the best claim or identifying holes in a claims library where new claims need to be introduced. One way to do this is through claims relationships [Chewar, 2005; Sutcliffe and Carroll, 1999; Wahid et al., 2011], formal statements associated with claims that point to related claims. These relationships can be built around similarities (e.g., claims that solve the same problem as in Sutcliffe's claims families [Sutcliffe, 2002], claims that build on each other during the design process [Wahid et al., 2004], or claims that mitigate downsides from the original claim [Wahid et al., 2004]).

It becomes more expedient to identify relationships among claims when they are associated with some sort of rating. A claims rating can capture opinions of designers or results from usability studies. One example of this is the critical parameter ratings explored by Chewar [2005]. These ratings provided three 0-1 numbers reflecting the low-high degree to which the claim supports the parameters of interruption, reaction, and comprehension. These ratings can come from expert review [Chewar, 2005] or can be calculated based on observed performance with interfaces that capture the claim [Chewar et al., 2004b]. By specifying these ratings within the claim, it becomes possible to search for claims with specified ratings, visually group claims with similar ratings, and construct claims that target a given rating.

One frequently cited drawback of many design rationale approaches is that they stifle creativity among designers, to the degree that it became the focus of a two-part journal special issue that explored how rationale and creativity can be linked [Carroll, 2010, 2011]. To ensure that claims (and other design rationale) does not stifle innovation, it is important to note that the tools and techniques we use to create and process claims are an integral part of what a claim is and how and when it is used. Our initial lack of success with a purely textual claims library (an ordered list of claims) encouraged us to explore how tools could help designers find, compare, and reuse claims [Chewar, 2005]. Our LINK-UP tool encourages claims-centered activities toward connecting and elaborating claims in design [Chewar et al., 2004a]. And establishment of collections of claims—positioned on a map, graph, or other visual display—provide design teams with choices in their design decision points, resulting in different design paths.

If the goal of a design session is to provide creative avenues for early speculation and brainstorming with each claim, then it seems counterintuitive to require participants to understand a claims library before undertaking their design activities. As such, tools and techniques associated with the claims library should provide ways to glean the sense of the claims quickly and easily, while providing avenues to understand more fully the claim when brainstorming shifts to a pruning stage. One way we have accomplished this is through the use of images associated with each claim, to encourage participants to form their own judgements and explore their own possibilities regarding the implications of the claim (and particularly the claim artifact) in design [Wahid, 2011]. Designers who first encounter a collection of images representing a claim library tend to be more creative in their design efforts than those given a text-only library [Chewar, 2005; Wahid, 2011]. The claims knowledge should still be available, but should be hidden until the designer needs additional prompting or feels ready to move from speculative creation to scientific defense of ideas. Our investigation into images and claims demonstrated much more creativity when images were shown first, with other claims knowledge initially hidden by the information presentation style [Wahid et al., 2009]. As seen with these approaches, the way that claims are presented to a design team suggests (and to some degree forces) a specific path that designers follow when using claims—resulting in some claims information being seen early on in the design process, some much later, and perhaps some never being seen.

## 1.3 BOOK OVERVIEW

The remainder of this book explores the evolution of claims, including examples of claims in use.

Chapter 2 examines knowing and sharing with a historical look at some of the key contributing instances related to knowledge generation during the design process, group participation and contribution to design efforts, and creation and use of design rationale.

Chapter 3 traces the evolution of claims—a look at the key evolution stages of claims in the field of human-computer interaction, from their introduction in the classic 1989 Carroll and Kellogg paper through three books that provided similar but importantly different views of claims, rooted in scientific inquiry, design engineering, and usability education.

Chapter 4 examines claims in engineering, science, and design for HCI—a series of case studies that look at this book author's experiences with claims in design efforts rooted in engineering, science, and design.

Chapter 5 looks forward to what claims can do—providing a speculative view of ways that claims will be useful for designers across disciplines in years moving forward, including ways that the nature of claims may need to change to make them easier to create and use, more accessible, and less suggestive.

Appendix A provides a timeline view of the evolution of claims, patterns, and issues. In the spirit of this book, it does this by generating a claim about each of 20 landmark works—a key feature from it, a few upsides and downsides, a narrative, and an exemplary picture or table.

# CHAPTER 2

# Knowing and Sharing

## FOUNDATIONAL EFFORTS

This chapter seeks to highlight foundational efforts of knowing and sharing, describing the foundations from which claims emerged as a knowledge capture and sharing unit for design in human-computer interaction (HCI). In so doing, this chapter chronologically explores four approaches that have had impact in the area: Paul Otlet's Mundaneum for knowledge extraction and sharing, Stephen Toulmin's claims-centered argumentation structure, Horst Rittel's issues and issue-based information system (IBIS), and Christopher Alexander's patterns of design. Each of these approaches emerged in the last century, as advances in knowledge and technology together inspired these visionaries in their quest to capture knowledge in a way that it could be shared, used, and reused in the pursuit of greater knowledge through design.

It was difficult to decide upon the four selected approaches, given the large number of influential people who have affected the area of HCI, particularly from design and argumentation perspectives. Much of the literature points to Aristotle and Plato as the first to explore deeply argumentation and rhetoric. Francis Bacon, the father of modern science and scientific inquiry, sought to capture and integrate knowledge in ways that would facilitate further idea generation. Herb Simon suggested a need to explore the specification and evaluation of artifacts, toward the creation of a "science of design". In contrast, researchers like Donald Schön and Lucy Suchman describe a more action-centric view of design, separate from a machine-like treatment of human action. A great many explorations of HCI provide the breadth of connection and contribution of these people and their ideas, toward applying these ideas to HCI and related domains (or toward suggesting alternative approaches) [Bacon, 1970; Carroll and Rosson, 1992; Flyvjbjerg, 2001; Pries-Heje and Baskerville, 2008; Schön, 1983; Simon, 1996]. While this work leverages those ideas, the focus is on providing an in-depth analysis of four knowledge-centric approaches, selected because of their connections to technology, their focus on knowledge structure, and their past and continuing relevance to important problems of knowing and sharing.

The remainder of this chapter explores the four selected approaches in detail. Section 2.1 talks about the vision of Paul Otlet and his Mundaneum, a collection of knowledge "chunks" from the early 20th century. Section 2.2 discusses Toulmin's argument structure and his articulation of a claim, which is often pointed to as the starting point for modern argumentation and design rationale. Section 2.3 examines the 1960s "new generation of design" methods, with 2.3.1 delving into the concept of wicked problems and issue-based information systems—relating issues to the notion of claims—and 2.3.2 examining design patterns and their impact on software engineering and HCI.

Section 2.4 positions claims within the space of argumentation approaches, with a detailed analysis of relative advantages and disadvantages compared to issues and patterns. Many of the examples from this chapters are captured as claims in Appendix A and are labeled as such throughout the chapter and the book (e.g., Toulmin's *claim* is in A.1).

## 2.1   OTLET'S EARLY VISION OF KNOWLEDGE DISSEMINATION

Researchers in CS and HCI love to point to Vannevar Bush as the father of all things Internet and Web related [Bush, 1945]. But even academic fathers have fathers themselves who set the stage for their ideas. Paul Otlet can be viewed in that role: a visionary from the early 1900s with a functional search engine—and a plan for an electronic interface to visualize the interconnections in knowledge. More importantly, he carefully considered how knowledge should be structured to best enable rapid understanding and easy sharing.

In the early decades of the 20th century, Otlet established a "Mundaneum"[1], a knowledge repository consisting of millions of facts drawn from the literature of the time. His work was inspired by Melvil Dewey and his Dewey Decimal System for classifying the knowledge so that it could be easily searched and compared. If you wanted to "Google" something in the early 20th century, you could "Otlet" it—mail in your request with a small fee, and get back 1 or 5 or 20 or 50 "hits" in response, each on a 3x5 card. He envisioned indexing all knowledge across different media, with access through a phone/screen interface supporting the comparison of many interrelated sources.

One could compare Otlet's Mundaneum to the World Wide Web, in its efforts to create a interconnected knowledge base. Somewhat ignored, but in many ways equally relevant and important to the workings of the Web, was Otlet's structuring of information on the cards. A key element of Otlet's vision resides in knowledge capture not at the level of a document, but at the level of the individual information chunks within the document. It is at this level that Otlet created interconnections between knowledge, such that no one piece of knowledge was an end point but rather a hub to other information. He classified information chunks into four categories: facts, interpretation of facts (opinions?), statistics, and sources. The chunks were linked and ranked in various ways—by topic, by public opinion, by Universal Decimal Classification—into a linked web-like "réseau" that aspired to be informational and social. Much like the chunks of knowledge returned from a Google search (including resource name and URL, number and time of prior visits, text from the resource deemed to be relevant, and relevant other search terms), Otlet's information chunk itself (without pursuing the originating book or media source) could provide the knowledge needed by the person doing the search.

There's a number of good Otlet and Otlet-related books and papers out there. A couple that appealed to me: New York Times editor Alex Wright's highly readable book *Glut* [Wright, 2007] has a large section overviewing Otlet's work (in the context of other information management efforts),

---

[1]Mundaneum may seem like an unfortunate name; but its goal to capture all human knowledge hearkens to the "earthly" sense of the word mundane, not the "ordinary" or "banal" sense.

and Boyd Rayward and his colleagues have written a number of books and articles on Otlet, including one that looks at his impacts on computer interfaces [Rayward, 2003; van den Heuvel and Rayward, 2011].

Alas, Otlet was quite popular and well supported in his home country of Belgium for a while, but died in poverty in 1944 after watching his collection be shifted into increasingly smaller quarters then be carted away by the Nazis. He was a major figure in knowledge capture and sharing for several decades though (much longer than, say, Google has been around!). The Mundaneum collapsed in part due to the explosion of information that was to be cataloged. And before you smugly say that such a thing will never happen in this digital age to the Googles of the world, consider whether it is truly possible to index and cross-reference and describe and meaningfully collect user opinion on every word and phrase and pixel and individual utterance in every document and video and security camera and satellite image and telescopic image that is collected. And if that's not possible, where do we draw the line? And if the current leaders choose the wrong line, there will surely be a next technology—the next Google—to fill the void.

## 2.2    TOULMIN, CLAIMS, AND ARGUMENTATION

The notion of a claim as a key element in design rationale entered the field of interaction design and human-computer interaction through Carroll and Kellogg's 1989 CHI paper. In that paper, they describe a claim as the psychological effects (positive and negative) that are caused by an artifact. They outline how claims can be used to guide design through the development and understanding of goals, plans, actions, and evaluation.

But certainly the roots of design rationale predate this artifact paper. Notably, Stephen Toulmin's classic *The Uses of Argument* [Toulmin, 1958]—the book that several researchers (e.g., Burge, 2005; Sutcliffe, 2002) point to as the seminal point in argumentation and design rationale— introduces the notion of a claim as a key part of argumentation. Similar to Carroll and Kellogg [1989] in their introduction of claims into the field of HCI, Toulmin spends large stretches of his book noting that claims are interesting because they are falsifiable—they may be true, but perhaps not, and must be re-evaluated as context changes. For example, Toulmin [1958, p.220] makes the summative statement that "we may accept over-hastily the suggestion that a claim to knowledge that proves mistaken must have been an improper claim" as the benefit comes from the creation and analysis inherent to claims. He criticizes our (very human) need for "a God's-eye view" that is universally true and instead encourages us to embrace the uncertainty as method.

Toulmin's *claim* is a conclusion for which a person must create a convincing argument. The claim must be supported by *evidence* (also called *ground* or *data*) that provides support for the claim. The claim and evidence are connected with a *warrant*. In an example from his book, a claim would be "Harry is a British citizen", supported by the evidence "Harry was born in Bermuda" and connected by the warrant "A person born in Bermuda will legally be a British citizen". (See a box-and-arrow layout of his argument in A.1.) Many arguments can be presented using these components, while others require three additional Toulmin components of backing (support for a warrant), rebuttal (restrictions on the claim), and qualifiers (reflections of the certainty of a claim). Continuing the example, one could rebut the claim by noting that "Harry could have become a naturalized U.S. citizen" or "Harry could have lost his citizenship for spying", which might require a "probably" or "almost certainly" qualifier for the claim, or additional backing for the warrant, or additional evidence in support of the claim.

As described in the preface to the 2003 edition of his *The Uses of Argument*, Toulmin notes that the book originally was meant to "criticize the assumption...that any significant argument can be put in formal terms". Instead, he ended up with a work that "expound[ed] a theory of rhetoric or argumentation" in a way he calls "informal" but actually seems more analytical. Although Toulmin originally targeted his argumentation structure as a counter to formal logic (e.g., in courtroom situations), Toulmin developed and expounded it for the fields of rhetoric and argumentation, summarized in Toulmin et al. [1979]. Other books have operationalized Toulmin's argumentation structure in more digestible and learner-friendly form, such as Booth's *The Craft of Research* [Booth et al., 1995]. It is somewhat ironic that it seems people now view the Toulmin method (and the methods based on it) as too formal and rigid—but it has been quite influential to the notions behind Carroll's scenario-based design and the IBIS-based methods and tools that I discuss in a later section of this chapter.

Alas, Toulmin is now dead. I mention that because he hasn't been dead for long (since 2009)—although many people assume that the person who wrote the 1958 classic book has been dead for many decades. In the preface of the 2003 edition of his book, he notes as much through a great story in which a person was shocked to find him alive (one of many such stories, it seems). Just as Toulmin points to Aristotle, Descartes, Wittgenstein, and other scientists and philosophers as the masterminds behind the concepts he espouses, Toulmin's work has influenced award-winning scholars and researchers like Wayne Booth, Douglas Walton, Donald Schön, Alistair Sutcliffe, and many others.

## 2.3   RITTEL, WICKED PROBLEMS, AND ISSUE-BASED INFORMATION SYSTEMS

The Issue-Based Information System (IBIS) approach to capturing and using design rationale is one of the leading design theories that addresses how groups identify, structure, and make decisions during the problem-solving process. IBIS was conceived by Horst Rittel in the 1970s as a way to deal with what he called *wicked problems*: unique and novel problems with no stopping rule or "right" answer. (See A.2 for an IBIS claim.) Wicked problems are commonly found in areas like climate change or road construction, where any solution that is undertaken will change the nature of the problem. HCI is rich with examples of wicked problems, particularly in situations where technology is introduced into a situation for which it might introduce distraction; e.g., map-based navigation systems in cars that can help people find an address in an unfamiliar area but that might distract them from the road.

Rittel's ideas about wicked problems and IBIS were borne as part of a "new generation" movement for design, posited by Rittel and his colleagues of the 1950s, including Archer, Jones, Asimow, and Alexander (described in Branham, 2009; Branham et al., 2010). This movement shifted away from the objective, rational approach to design to one that acknowledged the inherent intertwining of problem and solution, whereby engaging with a solution can affect the problem.

IBIS was the first of many argumentation-based solutions—spawning or directly influencing instantiations that include PHI, QOC, DRL, gIBIS, and Compendium—with a common trait that outlining the problem space is equivalent to outlining the solution space. (See A.6 for a claim about PHI and the PHIDIAS tool that instantiates it.) This section outlines the evolution of these design approaches, briefly exploring some key questions about when these approaches are (and are not) well suited, particularly for the field of human-computer interaction.

## 2.3.1   RITTEL, IBIS, AND IBIS-RELATED APPROACHES TO DESIGN

Rittel is often pointed to as the initiator of design rationale, stemming from a series of papers from the early 1970s to the early 1980s. Rittel and Webber [1973] laid out an extensive definition for wicked problems, featuring ten distinguishing properties of wicked problems (though Rittel and his colleagues had been discussing the issue and postulating approaches for at least five years prior to the paper). A Kunz and Rittel [1970] paper suggested that the right approach to address wicked problems was through *issues*, situationally dependent questions that are "raised, argued, settled, 'dodged', or substituted" during a design session. Rittel's concept of an issue is core to his Issue-Based Information Systems (IBIS) approach to group design and decision making, in which issues start a questioning process that links each issue with facts, positions, arguments, and other structures through knowledge relationships. The result is a knowledge space that does not solve the issue, but rather creates an environment of support and planning where people better understand each others' points of view. Rittel viewed IBIS as an approach to create an issue-centered information resource that would help people keep track of the topics raised in a discussion; in short, an approach to help them do as well as possible in decision-making.

IBIS provided a starting point for the many automated tools and methods that leveraged the IBIS argument-based nature and tree-like structure while simplifying or eliminating many of its vagaries and complexities. The first widely used and publicized tool was gIBIS, a graphical IBIS tool developed and popularized in the 1990s by Jeff Conklin and his collaborators [Begeman and Conklin, 1988; Conklin and Yakemovic, 1988], and its follow-up tool QuestMap [Conklin and Yakemovic, 1991]. (See A.4 for a gIBIS claim and screenshot.) Conklin's work stemmed from his involvement with the Microelectronics and Computer Technology Corporation (MCC), a consortium of companies seeking to identify ways to develop software efficiently [Belady and Richter, 1985]. Conklin engaged with Horst Rittel to learn about IBIS, adapting it for use in software engineering.

Rittel's student Ray McCall leveraged the tree-like hypertext structure of IBIS in his Procedural Hierarchy of Issues (PHI), extending the IBIS model based on a more complete model of design and on his extensive experience with IBIS [McCall, 1989, 1991]. The PHI model of design includes a broader view of issues, with support for more ways to raise, relate, and resolve issues. PHI is supported in hyptertext tools for computer-aided design and decision-making, including PRO-TOCOL, MIKROPLIS, PHIDIAS, and JANUS [Fischer et al., 1989; McCall, 1989; McCall et al., 1990; McCall, 1991; McCall et al., 1992; Schuler and Smith, 1990].

Other approaches to design rationale management drew inspiration from this early IBIS/PHI work: Questions, Options, and Criteria (QOC) by Maclean et al. [1996]; and Lee's [1991] Decision Representation Language (DRL), extending the work of Potts and Bruns [1988]. QOC focused specifically on the *artifacts* being designed, framing the issues of IBIS as questions about artifacts that must be addressed through options and decision criteria. The focus of DRL is on *decisions*, not the broader concept of design addressed by IBIS, with consideration for the goals, alternatives, groups, and claims (facts) that contribute to the decision-making process. Much of the reflective literature on design rationale groups these three techniques together, with Dutoit et al. noting that "there are so few significant differences in the schemas of IBIS, QOC, and DRL"—although there's an excellent detailing of the differences in the opening chapter of the book [Dutoit et al., 2006].

### 2.3.2   COMPENDIUM

Emerging from the IBIS and the IBIS-like approaches of the 1980s and 1990s was a need for community involvement in the design and use of these tools and their associated techniques— for practitioners to evolve them through use in a variety of situations. One such effort resulted in the Compendium system, an IBIS-inspired hypermedia mapping tool created by a consortium of universities and research labs in Europe and the U.S. It is rooted in Rittel's wicked problem conceptualization and IBIS approach to design and design rationale capture, building on combined efforts of Al Selvin, Simon Buckingham Shum, Jeff Conklin, and many others. Compendium allows designers to create a node-link graph of interrelated concepts, including questions, ideas, pros and cons, references, and decisions. It is similar to mind map tools, though it explicitly seeks to integrate many opinions rather than implicitly focusing on a single "mind".

Unlike most of the other IBIS-related approaches and tools that emerged from universities or research labs, Compendium evolved at Nynex, largely through the efforts of Al Selvin[2] and Maarten Sierhuis. Selvin and his colleagues began using conversational modeling tools, initially from others but starting in 1998 of their own creation, in an effort to create tools that would be used repeatedly (and not abandoned, as often happened) in the software design process.

Compendium emerged in 1998 and 1999, with a growing consortium of contributions from the Center for Creative Leadership (CCL) and the Knowledge Media Institute (KMi), along with Selvin's company (of changing names—originally Nynex, then Bell Atlantic, and currently Verizon). Together, Selvin and numerous other researchers and practitioners with significant experience in IBIS-inspired approaches—Simon Buckingham Shum, Maarten Sierhuis, Jeff Conklin, Michelle Bachler, and others—to create the most current and widely-used instantiation of the IBIS ideas in

---

[2]See Selvin's series of blog posts about the beginnings of Compendium starting at www.knowledgeart.blogspot.com/2008/10/more-compendium-history-part-1.html.

the Compendium dialog mapping tool. In 2003, Selvin worked with Verizon to allow the Open University to freely distribute the software and code for Compendium. A team at KMi—including Selvin, who made Compendium central to his Ph.D. work at KMi from 2003–2012—has worked to evolve and maintain Compendium for an active user community.

Compendium is best suited for a trained and experienced facilitator who leads a synchronous, co-located group in a decision-making activity [Culmsee, 2012]. (See Compendium claims at A.11 and A.20.) An experienced facilitator should smoothly handle even the most disgruntled and undirected group, prompting them to introduce unresolved issues, probing for alternate ideas to core problems, asking for additional questions to maintain a set of well-considered ideas. The result should be a knowledge tree in which the participants understand the core problems and the concerns of each member of the group. The participants are not "done" thinking about the problems, and there will not necessarily be a clear path for moving forward, but everyone should have had the opportunity to share and comment on the elements of the Compendium tree.

There are challenges for untrained novices getting started with Compendium[3]—even (especially!) with the 42-page getting-started manual. There's also a 2-page quick reference sheet as well, but it is most helpful once one has a basic understanding of Compendium's purpose and core functionality. There are the typical "starting-with-a-blank-slate" problems where the initial actions aren't obvious (e.g., click and drag behaviors to create nodes, right click and drag to link nodes). And the layout only supports graphs of about 20–30 nodes before it becomes impossible to simultaneously read the labels and view the entire graph (due also to the lack of good zoom options or automated graph layouts).

There are lots of upsides to the tool, beginning with a quality search feature. Embedded node information can be found through the search, and it is possible to extend the search to include deleted nodes. The node-link layout is easy to manipulate with a little practice. It is possible to save graphs in a reloadable XML format or a view-only HTML format (though it does not seem possible for distributed groups to simultaneously edit a Compendium graph). Other features like history and a complex undo-redo seem to be under way, but there is no clear timeline for the completion of those features.

For further reading, the previously-cited book chapter "Hypermedia support for argumentation-based rationale: 15 years on from gIBIS and QOC" and the case study in the more recent *Human Technology* journal describe the history and uses of Compendium Buckingham et al. [2006]; Selvin et al. [2010]. Jeff Conklin authored a book titled *Dialogue Mapping* [2005] that includes a tutorial-style view of identifying wicked problems and employing Compendium to deconstruct them. Finally, the book *The Heretics Guide to Best Practices* [Culmsee and Awati, 2011], authored by a consultant and an information systems manager, provides motivation and framing of wicked problems, copious examples of Compendium in business and consulting situations, in-depth history of Compendium, and both positive and negative examples of Compendium's utility. The

---

[3]The author's experiences using Compendium are detailed www.mccricks.wordpress.com/2011/10/07/compendium-review/.

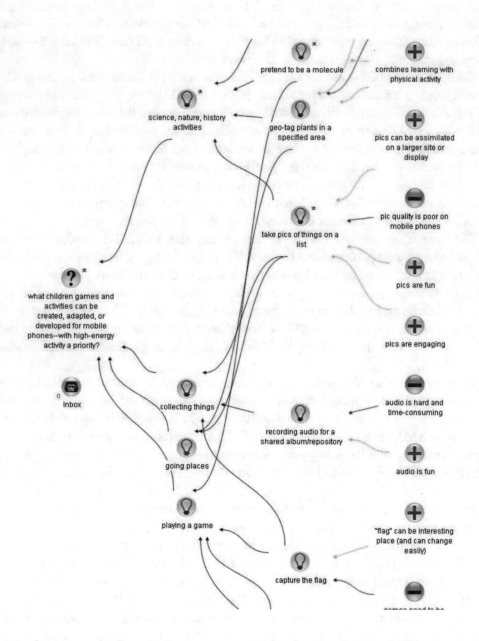

**Figure 2.1:** A portion of a Compendium tree, containing a question (indicated with a question mark icon), ideas (light bulb), and pluses and minuses for the ideas.

Compendium web site[4] provides free downloads and access to a listserv for anyone who registers at the site. And finally, two claims in Appendix A (A.11 and A.20) are about Compendium.

In summary, the big issues with Compendium related to scalability and history: it's hard to see more than a dozen nodes at once, and support for rolling back to previous views was limited. But it's much more usable than gIBIS, and it seems to have attracted a fairly sizable following among usability consultants. Features like scalability and history don't seem to be a focus of the Compendium tool. In fact, it seems that the biggest contribution of Compendium is not in how knowledge is represented (which had been done before) or in how it is manipulated (simplified...or in some cases ignored or deferred to a future version of the tool), but in the social processes around how the tool is used: an expert in knowledge management and the IBIS/Compendium provides real-time guidance during the analysis process, toward helping the participants debate directions moving forward.

Looking forward, the continued development of the Compendium tool is driven by KMi, and as such is dependent on its possible research objectives (and accompanying research funding). The KMi team actively uses Compendium, and the Compendium mailing list has received over a hundred emails over the five months from October 2011 to February 2012, so there are others who use it and build on its ideas as well. There seems to be interest in spinning off other development efforts, but it is unclear when or whether that will happen.

### 2.3.3  REFLECTIONS ON IBIS-RELATED SOLUTIONS

In summary, two related trends that I notice in these IBIS-based tools are that (1) the "hard" stuff is left for experts; and (2) the approaches seek more immediate value to designers. Perhaps this is a response to a shift from academia to consultant environments—consultants certainly need to carve out an "expert" role for themselves, and they'd better make sure there's value to the participants at the end of the day.

Another trend from IBIS to QOC to gIBIS to Compendium is that the approaches seem to be increasingly question-driven—as opposed to issue-driven—with progressively fewer structuring options for the knowledge that is generated. The early Rittel definition of *issue* positions it as something "brought up and disputed because different positions are assumed" [Kunz and Rittel, 1970]. In contrast, a *question* is interrogative, suggesting that an answer is forthcoming (rather than a debate).

Is there a path of simplification and certainty in the IBIS approach and tools—contrary to the original "wicked problem" mandate that problems don't have solutions, merely different states of being? Or does the simplification actually match the vision of wickedness that Rittel initially posed? Part of the definition of wicked problems is that there is no stopping rule, but certainly it was not Rittel's intent that we debate issues indefinitely. As such, some sort of path to simplicity (a taming of wicked problems) is necessary.

---

[4]www.compendium.open.ac.uk/institute/

The shift to a question-driven approach is part of a focus on ease of use and understanding of the IBIS approach, in response to negative reactions by users. The complexity of many of the early IBIS-based approaches meant that they were too confusing or time-consuming to use in practical applied design settings (e.g., Buckingham, 1996; Halasz, 1988; Selvin, 2011). The later tools tended to be less intrusive than the original IBIS approach (i.e., less formality, resulting in simpler structures) with more prescriptive outcomes (including specific solutions). Also, the later tools emphasized the importance of a trained and experienced practitioner to facilitate an outcome-driven process. This simpler model enabled more immediate value to the participants, for whom value from the tool was imperative for any time investment (e.g., Buckingham et al., 2006; Conklin, 2005; Conklin et al., 2001; Selvin, 1999, 2011). In later sections we note a similar trend from minimally used complex tools to more widely used simple tools for claims-based approaches to design.

One big drawback I see with many of these approaches is that they can create a false sense of certainty in a world of changing truth, change that occurs in most design efforts and is prominent in the field of HCI. That's a point of concern with Compendium and other tools (regarding scalability and history) in which problem spaces become more complex over time. Lots of factors—the state of technology, the skill sets of the designers, the knowledge, skills, and acceptance levels of the target user population—change over time, and decisions that were made at any single point may not apply later. Revisiting two key feature of wicked problems: solutions (or problem states) aren't right or wrong, and there's no stopping rule. Popper, as paraphrased in the seminal Rittel and Webber [1973] paper, suggested that solutions to problems should only be posited as "hypotheses offered for refutation;" otherwise, you can end up pursuing tame solutions to wicked problems. Toulmin, in one of his later books *Cosmopolis*, similarly argues that solutions to problems must be developed situationally, in his "return to the timely" argument [Toulmin, 1992].

Finally, we must be careful that we're not reducing the wickedness of a problem to the creation of a claims map, or the mapping of a dialog, or the removal of storms from brains—in effect, turning the wicked problem into a tame one. Or, if we choose to do that, we must ensure that, when a design team goes back to look at a DR representation, each element in it is appropriately questioned. Sometimes computer tools can hurt in that regard—they help designers violate some tenet of wickedness by providing a "memory" that captures truths that don't exist, or by encouraging the capture of knowledge at the wrong granularity.

Two writings that elaborate historical review are Hypermedia Support for Argumentation-Based Rationale: 15 Years on from gIBIS and QOC by Buckingham et al. [2006], and *Rationale Management in Software Engineering: Concepts and Techniques* edited by Dutoit et al. [2006]. A great many more readings were highly influential and enlightening: the classic *Design Rationale* book by Moran and Carroll [1996] that captured the state-of-the-art for the design rationale field, the recent pair of special issues of the *Human Technology* journal on Creativity and Rationale in Software Design [Carroll, 2010, 2011], and views and approaches centered around wicked problems and IBIS found in blog posts and white papers of dedicated practitioners including Paul Culmsee, Kailash Awati, Jeff Conklin, and Al Selvin.

# 2.4    ALEXANDER, PATTERNS, AND PATTERN LANGUAGES

*Patterns* seek to capture the most important aspects of a solution to a recurring design problem, such that they can be repurposed or reused in similar problems. Patterns originated in the architecture community and have spread to technology-related disciplines, including computer science and human-computer interaction. Interaction design patterns are viewed as useful because they can represent optimal or near-optimal solutions for some class of activity [Cooper and Reimann, 2003]. Different communities have established their own definitions for the key elements and formatting of a pattern, although Wania [2008] notes that there is some agreement that patterns should include a problem, its context, and a solution. This section explores the evolution of patterns, how and why they were adopted by the HCI community and its subcommunities, and ongoing and future directions for patterns.

Christopher Alexander introduced the concept of a pattern in the domain of architecture and urban planning in the 1970s [Alexander, 1979; Alexander et al., 1977], as an alternative to Rittel's conceptualization of issues and IBIS. Both Alexander and Rittel were part of the early search for new ways for thinking about design, but Alexander's conceptualization of patterns represented an opposing view to how to think about design: Rittel's issues and IBIS encouraged a lack of commitment and a constant rethinking of the problem, while Alexander's patterns provided detailed views of solutions meant to be timeless and broadly applicable to many problems within a domain.

Alexander's patterns describe a solution to a commonly occurring problem in urban architecture; for example, a "Beer Hall" should address the need for hundreds of people to connect with each other by providing large tables for groups in the center of a space, an open area for individuals and small group mingling around the edges, with other areas for dancing and darts and such. (A claim about patterns can be found in A.3.) Each pattern typically includes a multi-page description, with references to other co-located patterns; Alexander's collection of 253 interconnected patterns made up what he termed a *pattern language* [Alexander et al., 1977], in which most patterns point to other patterns that support or complement them in some way.

Patterns were adapted for software engineering during the 1990s, highlighted by a pattern collection "gang of four" [Gamma et al., 1995]. These patterns focused on suggested code structures that promote desirable behavior of the software. Much of the book focuses on the presentation of 23 software design patterns, supported by techniques for conducting object-oriented design and programming in a way that leverages patterns. The pattern are grouped in areas—with only a few connections between them—creating more of a pattern collection or categorization than a true language. (See a claim about "gang of four" patterns in A.8.)

The mid- to late-1990s also saw the start of many software engineering patterns conferences and workshops—such as PLoP and its regional spinoffs (e.g., EuroPLoP, NordicPLoP, ChiliPLop), the Pervasive Patterns Conference, and others. Some of these conferences have included tracks on patterns for human-computer interaction and interface design, and the PLoP Conference featured one of the first large patterns languages for HCI—a 50-pattern collection of *interaction design patterns* by Tidwell [1998]. The collection was shepherded by John Vlissides (of the Gang of Four) with help credited to software engineering and HCI notables Jim Coplien and Tom Erickson, among others.

The patterns conferences typically consist of tight-knit groups of people who mix idea exchange with team building. The conferences often have some sort of shepherding component, allowing experienced pattern writers and users to assist their colleagues in crafting a useful pattern—but also in creating an interpersonal bond among those authoring the patterns and those shepherding the process. It is this connection among patterns practitioners that fuels the continuation of these types of conferences—and, I would argue, the process of authoring a pattern that has as much, or more, value than the completed patterns themselves.

Patterns were explored by the HCI community through workshops and panels starting in the late 1990s (e.g., Bayle et al., 2008; Borchers and Thomas, 2001; Fincher et al., 2003). The focus of these workshops shifted from exploratory efforts to define roles for patterns in HCI to more in-depth efforts that sought to populate patterns libraries. The earliest workshop [Bayle et al., 2008] described two types of interaction patterns: *activity patterns* that are descriptive of the current state of an interface; and *design patterns* that connect a common problem with a proven solution—identifying a claims-like means to explore hypotheses about the current state of things in addition to the traditional patterns approach to identify established "truths". (See A.9 for a claim about activity and design patterns, and an example from the workshop.) This workshop, and the subsequent ones, identified many ways of using patterns, both prescriptive ways that captured and generalized existing solutions in a *lingua franca* meant to be accessible to future designers, and predictive ways meant to encourage exploration (and possible rejection) of ideas based on further research and exploration.

Workshops dedicated primarily to patterns at the large, broad HCI conferences like ACM SIGCHI, INTERACT, and CSCW ended in the early- to mid-1990s, reportedly because the workshop chairs felt there had been enough of a focus on patterns per se. However, within HCI-related fields there continue to be workshops in focused areas that have sought to create patterns libraries (e.g., Luyten et al., 2010, 2011; Schummer et al., 2004). They adopted similar practices of shepherding, categorization, and group discussion and bonding that is common to the software engineering community. But looking more broadly than these efforts from HCI subdisciplines, there does not seem to be the broad response to the call for patterns from the ACM SIGCHI community in the late 1990s and early 2000s. The numerous books and web sites, generally authored by one or a small group of researchers and practitioners, fill an important niche for areas like web design, interactive exhibits, mobile interfaces, and interactive TV. But there seem to be opportunities for other design approaches, both to contribute to a community-oriented evolving design repository and to provide easy-to-understand design knowledge that can be readily applied by diverse design teams—whether through issues, claims, or other instantiations of patterns.

A great many books released starting in the early 2000s built on these early successes in the HCI domain. Jan Borchers, building on his dissertation work and his participation in many of the CHI workshops, panels, and other related efforts, provided the first collection of patterns for HCI [Borchers, 2001], in which he describes key elements of patterns for interaction design and provides three pattern languages for interactive exhibits. van Duyne et al. [2002] created a book of web design patterns that evolved from early efforts of their research group at Berkeley. Tidwell expanded her patterns web site for interaction design into a book that was first published in 2005 and updated in 2010 [Tidwell, 2005]. Many of these books have associated web sites, often with tools that help users navigate, group, and sort the patterns. In addition, there are many other patterns web sites; widely-used and frequently-updated ones include Yahoo!'s design patterns library (`www.developer.yahoo.com/forum/`), the User Interface Design Pattern Library (`ui-patterns.com`), and Martijn van Welie's Patterns in Interaction Design (`www.welie.com/patterns`). For a comprehensive and growing list of pattern languages and resources, see Tom Erickson's Interaction Design Patterns Page at `www.visi.com/~snowfall/InteractionPatterns.html`.

Much of the evidence that patterns are an effective tool for design comes from designers' and researchers' anecdotal experiences with them, with the creators of patterns libraries arguing that a quality pattern is exemplified by positive resolution of an established problem with minimal side effects [Alexander, 1979; Wania, 2008]. Researchers have suggested that three positive examples are sufficient to confirm the validity of a pattern [Lafreniere and Hedenskog, 2001]. In addition, a handful of empirical evaluations of patterns point primarily to the benefits of increased communication among designers who use patterns, with little revealed regarding increased quality or efficiency of design [Abraham, 2011; Abraham and Atwood, 2009; Borchers, 2001; Chung et al., 2004; Dearden and Finlay, 2006; Wania, 2008]. From these studies, it seems that most of the patterns libraries rely on expert analysis with little or no empirical basis—factors that should be taken into account when considering whether to use patterns and patterns libraries. However, the opinions and experiences of experts are quite important—these evaluation results certainly do not suggest that we should discount patterns as a design approach.

Recent and ongoing patterns efforts largely have focused on two areas: applying patterns language creation to focused areas, and exploring ways to make patterns more accessible. New conferences in emerging areas often use pattern creation as a way to identify key truths within the domain libraries (e.g., Luyten et al., 2010, 2011; Schummer et al., 2004), and individuals often position their entry into a field in the form of a pattern or pattern language (e.g., Thomas, 2011, 2012). The expectation for these efforts seems to be that individuals bring patterns to a workshop, then collectively the attendees would work to improve the patterns.

Companies that do not use patterns cite a lack of time to integrate them into their design efforts [Hennipman et al., 2008]. To make patterns more accessible for designers, innovations like pre-patterns encourage early-stage pattern creation and use that is more hypothetical in nature [Chung et al., 2004; Saponas et al., 2006]. Researchers have turned to tool development, rather than just pattern innovation, to make it easier to find, use, and learn from patterns; for example, Geert van der Veer's Visual Design Course Pattern Wizard that leverages existing pattern languages from Tidwell and van Welie but adds tools to support pattern search, connection, and creation [Consiglio and van der Veer, 2011]. And emerging new guidelines for patterns—e.g., inclusion of images with all patterns, and creation of maps to show patterns connections—make it easier to grasp the meaning of individual patterns and to understand relationships among patterns. It is this focus on broad accessibility that portends wider use of patterns in a greater number of situations—while also opening up the possibility for more connections with other design approaches based on issues and claims.

# CHAPTER 3

# Evolution of Claims

## WHERE DID THEY COME FROM, WHERE DID THEY GO

This chapter seeks to trace the evolution of the claim in human-computer interaction (HCI), from its introduction in the Carroll and Kellogg [1989] paper through the appearance of three books, *Making Use* by John M. Carroll [2000], *The Domain Theory* by Alistair Sutcliffe [2002], and *Usability Engineering* by Rosson and Carroll [2002]. (Key contributions in claims, juxtaposed with contributions in patterns and issues, are shown chronologically in Appendix A.) The definition and role of "claims" shifted significantly during that time period; I'm seeking to identify some of the evolutionary shifts from 1989–2002. This list is not meant to be complete, but rather it seeks to highlight the most important evolutionary points in the conceptualization of the claim.

Three phases highlight the progress in this evolution:

1. Carroll and his colleagues at IBM T.J. Watson in the late 1980s and early 1990s. They were seeking ways to design not just toward creating a single design, but toward crafting a theory-based approach to design to enable designers to build on each others' work in a meaningful, scientific way. This work continued until Carroll left for Virginia Tech, at which time his focus largely shifted to collaborative computing (save for a few papers that seemed to draw on his IBM work).

2. Sutcliffe and Carroll's collaboration, highlighted by Sutcliffe's sabbatical time at Virginia Tech. Sutcliffe had been working for many years on knowledge abstraction in software design, and, like Carroll and his group, he was inspired by potential roles for theory in HCI.

3. Three summative works led by Carroll, Sutcliffe, and Rosson. Each presented a different view of the role of claims—in the fields of design, engineering, and education, respectively.

## 3.1 GROWING THE GARDEN

Claims were introduced to the field of HCI in Carroll and Kellogg's "Artifact as theory nexus" paper at CHI 1989 [Carroll and Kellogg, 1989]. They seemed to base their definition on Toulmin's 1958 use of the term [Toulmin, 1958], in which he established claims as a hypothesis-centered approach to crafting arguments. The Carroll and Kellogg paper seeks to move beyond the narrow focus of cognitive-based theories that were prominent in the 1980s (that focused on low-level phenomena like keystrokes) by introducing the a hermeneutic approach based on **psychological claims**, the effects on people of both natural and designed artifacts. Claims were the central part of a **task-analysis framework**, an attempt to position the design and interpretation of HCI artifacts as a central component of HCI research. This approach was intended to bridge the gap from research to innovation—reconciling the "hermeneutics vs. theory-based design" conflict in the title. Several examples in the paper showed how developing an understanding of a claim—the artifact *and* its possible effects—can point out how much we have to learn and can encourage us to draw broader conclusions. Many of these issues, in particular the connection of claims and claims analysis to the task-artifact cycle, is elaborated in Carroll and Moran [1991] paper, but the ideas were first presented in Carroll and Kellogg [1989].

A 1992 BIT paper [Carroll et al., 1992] provided the first in-depth view of the tech transfer of UE results (although see the Carroll and Moran [1991] special issue and 1996 book described below). It connected the Scriven view of **mediated evaluation** to claims upsides and downsides, positioning claims as a contributor in the field of design rationale. In so doing, it expounded upon claims as a way to reuse knowledge, by encouraging designer consideration of specialized vs abstract claims. The expectation was that designers could use claims to "avoid throwing away thoughtful empirical work". They avoided Grudin's paradox, stating outright that design rationale (including claims-centric design rationale) was not an automatic mechanism, but requires additional human thought to yield a reusable knowledge unit.

A 1992 TOIS article [Carroll and Rosson, 1992] opined that HCI should be an **action-science** "that produces 'knowledge-in-implementation' and views design practice as inquiry". The paper argues that the task-artifact cycle is an action-science because designers must respond to user requirements by building artifacts with upsides and downsides—i.e., claims. This paper distinguishes the scenario/claim roles as such: "Where scenarios are a narrative account, claims are a causal account". It argues that scenarios provided a situation narrative, but they are too rich, hard to classify, and hard to reuse (arguments brought up again and addressed to varying degrees by Chewar [2005]; Sutcliffe [2002], and others). It is the claim that establish the link to action-science by facilitating design analysis, providing a mechanism for generalization and hypothesis, and explicitly recognizing potential tradeoffs.

A 1994 IJHCS paper by Carroll et al. provided a **software-centric** scenario-based design approach, with Point-of-View (POV) scenarios drawing parallels to object-centric/object-oriented development. This paper represents the most process-based, engineering-focused, and software-generative view of scenario-based design—both until this time and thereafter. Although claims play a fairly minor role in this paper (only appearing in step 4, leveraging the upsides and downsides in analysis and hillclimbing), there seemed to be opportunity for a much larger role: identifying objects, specifying interactions between objects, supporting inheritance, etc. There was also initial discussion of an **education focus** for POV scenarios, SBD, claims, and such—but it was not elaborated, and Rosson and Carroll [2002] described a more simplified approach to teaching design. This paper seemed to be hypothesized starting points that were not fully pursued by the authors—rich for mining by Sutcliffe, Chewar, and others in the years to come.

Moran and Carroll's [1996] *Design Rationale* book (elaborated from their special issue of the *HCI Journal* Carroll and Moran, 1991) is pointed to as a landmark in the field of design rationale. It draws together contributions from Jintae Lee, Allan MacLean, Clayton Lewis, Simon Buckingham Shum, Gary Olson, Gerhard Fischer, Colin Potts, Jeff Conklin, Jonathan Grudin, and many others. Of relevance to the topic of claims is the introduction (by co-editors Tom Moran and Jack Carroll) and a Carroll and Rosson chapter. These chapters exhibit connections in their work to Horst Rittel (wicked problems, IBIS), Francis Bacon (deliberated evolution), Herb Simon (environment and behavior), and Donald Schön (contexts of experience)—putting forth the most synthesized view of the position of claims within the design community. Some of the psychological themes, particularly those of Simon, are elaborated in Carroll's [1997] journal paper in *Annual Reviews of Psychology*.

## 3.2 SOFTWARE ENGINEERING TO USABILITY ENGINEERING

Sutcliffe and Carroll [1999] summarize the joint efforts of the two authors on the use of claims as a **knowledge capture and reuse mechanism**. It delved into the possibility of using claims as a reuse mechanism, a concept touched upon in previous work but never described in sufficient detail. The paper introduced a formatting and classification scheme for claims (and scenarios) to enable their reuse, including a process and alternate pathways for claim evolution. Among the augmentations was the first explicit connection to its derivation history and background theory (i.e., where it came from), leading to the first claim map that can reflect parentage, original/evolving context, motivation, evidence, and possibilities for reuse. Also of great importance was the acknowledgement of work left to do: methods for indexing, tool support (hypertext links, structure matching), and the need for buy-in (and stay-in) incentives. (A claim about the Sutcliffe and Carroll claim, including an example, is in A.10.)

Sutcliffe's 2000 TOCHI paper seeks to address the irrelevance of HCI in industry, particularly with regard to a theory-based engineering approach. The paper seeks to identify ways to deliver HCI knowledge in a tractable form that is reusable across applications—and, more importantly, across application areas. The paper argues that claims could provide a bridge if **reuse scope** was improved; specifically, if there were generic versions of claims and artifacts, and if there were mechanisms for matching claims to new application contexts. The bulk of the paper provides a three-step process to accomplish this: steps for creating more generic claims, mechanisms for cross-domain reuse, and approaches to recognize broader implications. Parts of these are elaborated in Sutcliffe's book (described later) and in the dissertations of Chewar [2005] and Wahid [2011]. Other important products of this work are the notion of claim families, a claims-patterns comparison, and an explicit recognition of the importance of claims as "designer-digestible" knowledge (one of my favorite phrases).

## 3.3   DEFINITIONAL TEXTS

From the early years of claims evolution emerged three different visions featuring claims in HCI, featured in three books that appeared in the early 2000's: Carroll's *Making Use*, Sutcliffe's *The Domain Theory*, and Rosson and Carroll's *Usability Engineering*.

Carroll's [2000] *Making Use* book pulled together his vision for scenario-based design for scientists, with an eye toward the discovery process. The early parts of the book describe the complex, uncertain nature of design, leading to a proposition that scenario-based design can provide a simultaneously concrete and flexible approach to design that would encourage reflection and focus project orientation. Claims are used to augment the scenario-based design process, highlighting key aspects of the design (and leaving the generalization of claims as an exercise for the designer). Claims generally arise from the scenario creation process as a concrete concept, though the book also discusses *theory-based claims* as an abstract vision meant to be grounded in an instantiated artifact. Much of the value from claims comes from *claims analysis*, an inclusive term that covers any critical examination of one or more claims (e.g., participatory analysis, refactoring upsides and downsides, and stopping heuristics). The book also explores the future of claims, notably asking whether reuse desirable, given the overhead—a question addressed by Sutcliffe's book (described next) and by our own work discussed in Chapter 4.

Sutcliffe's [2002] *The Domain Theory* provides a reuse-centric view of software engineering, with a focus on abstracting the problem space into a framework that captures, records, and systematizes expert experiences into patterns for knowledge and software reuse. Patterns are the primary knowledge capture mechanism in Sutcliffe's domain theory to capture application classes and problem domain models, with claims used to capture rationale regarding conflicts encountered during the design process. The role of claims is to make concrete Domain Theory's high level of abstraction (too high, according to critics) by leveraging the high utility (but low flexibility and poor reuse) of claims. The book extends the formal claims schema discussed earlier in the chapter (from Sutcliffe and Carroll, 1999) with hypertext links to supporting material. This formal structure supports the creation of a library of claims, with the claims linked to each other and to domain models—thus supporting searching, browsing, and reuse.

Finally, Rosson and Carroll's [2002] *Usability Engineering* textbook advocates scenario-based development as a teaching tool, with claims and claims analysis a complementary and guiding technique to scenario development during each stage of design. In contrast to the Sutcliffe book, it presents claims in a simplified, stripped-down manner (for better and worse) meant to be highly accessible for students, particularly undergraduates. Also in contrast to the Sutcliffe book, the Rosson and Carroll book is not a fully defined engineering process. Rather, it leverages an overarching usability engineering process—using scenarios and claims as evolving knowledge capture and sharing mechanisms—as a gateway to situationally-appropriate scientific and engineering tools and methods (e.g., distributed cognition, Gestalt principles, empirical evaluations). An example of a claim from *Usability Engineering* is in A.12.

# 3.4   CONTINUING EVOLUTION OF CLAIMS

The three books in the prior section set forth three similar visions for the power and possibilities for claims in human-computer interaction. These books marked a certain level of maturity of ideas regarding claims—reflecting a willingness from the book authors to present the ideas to be used by HCI practitioners, researchers, and educators. But the use of claims, and indeed the notion of what a claim is, has continued to advance.

A great many research efforts in the years since these books appeared cite one or more of them (or one or more of their preceding papers) in critiquing, leveraging, extending, and applying the notion of claims to problems of HCI and related domains. Notable among the efforts is the work of Steven Haynes, who used scenarios and claims in the evaluation of collaborative systems [Haynes et al., 2004]. This work focuses on a specific type of claims analysis in which claims elicited from study participants are grouped into sets of positive and negative propositions, which are then used to assess envisioned and implemented designs. (See A.14 for more details and an example.) Haynes also uses claims as a brainstorming tool in workshops and classes, encouraging participants first to list out artifacts related to a topic, then to delve into the upsides and downsides of selected features—resulting in a small list of high quality ideas ready for prototyping and testing, and a much larger list of ideas that may be worth pursuing further. A great many others have employed claims throughout the design process, from early brainstorming to prototype design and implementation to evaluation.

The use of claims and scenarios in design is not without its criticisms, many stemming from the uncertain, non-quantifiable nature of the textual descriptions at the core of the representations (e.g., a claim downside that an interface artifact is "highly interruptive" has uncertain meaning with regard to user population, context, etc.). Notable among the criticisms was the reaction in a book review from Diaper [2002], who argued that scenarios and claims lack the ability to create a complete definition of a target interface, requiring a balance of creativity and attention to detail that is difficult to achieve. He suggests the use of *task analysis* methods as ways to encourage greater breadth of coverage and to provide potential stopping rules for design. Paternò [2002] extends Diaper's argument, stating that not just task analysis but *task modeling* is needed to bridge from the abstraction of scenarios and claims to capture the relationships between the chunks of knowledge in design. It has been argued that personas address limitations of claims and scenarios by creating a compelling, concrete character (generally an archetype with characteristics drawn from actual target users) with whom the designer can empathize [Cooper, 1999; Cooper and Reimann, 2003; Cooper et al., 2007; Grudin and Pruitt, 2002]. And other researchers explored the ways that scenarios could assist in connecting HCI to other disciplines, in particular software engineering [Benyon and Macaulay, 2002; Burge et al., 2008; Sutcliffe, 2006]. A key result of these and other debates and discussions was to extend the set of tools and techniques with connections to claims and scenarios—thus positioning for easy adoption and use the methods of scenario-based design and claims analysis within the space of design methods for HCI and related disciplines.

Many of the above examples sought to formalize the nature of claims and related approaches, toward creating a structured engineering approach to the design of interfaces. But there are examples where designers consider only a part of a claim, using them as a gateway to creative inspiration during the design process. For example, the work of Bill Gaver and his colleagues used the heart of a claim—the artifact—as a hypothetical nexus to explore design alternatives [Gaver and Martin, 2000]. They broaden the stated focus in Carroll and Kellogg [1989] on cognitive aspects of usability to look at questions of technology, aesthetics, and the psychological, social, and cultural effects of artifacts. Gaver's work balances the theoretical possibilities captured in an artifact with the possibilities that designers' perspectives can lend to the design effort.

Clearly, the meaning and purpose of a claim is not a settled issue—as should be the case for a discipline like HCI that is itself not yet well defined. Harkening back to the facets of HCI from the opening chapter, it is interesting to see how engineers, scientists, and creative designers have adopted the core ideas of claims to meet their purposes. The next chapter of this book provides an in-depth exploration of the author's experiences with claims from the perspectives of each of these facets. The final chapter provides a vision for the future, looking at how each of these facets—and other emerging themes in HCI—can continue to leverage, extend, and evolve the claim.

CHAPTER 4

# Using Claims

## ENGINEERING, SCIENCE, AND CREATIVE DESIGN

Human-computer interaction (HCI) draws from an increasing number of approaches to design, and, as a young discipline, it does not yet have well-established and widely accepted means for knowledge capture and dissemination. This book has discussed approaches to accomplish this, focusing on claims primarily but also discussing issues and patterns. This section discusses some of the relative merits of each approach—including how they can draw from each other, and what an effective knowledge capture approach might ultimately be like—and it presents examples of claims as they have been used in design situations.

For the purposes of this discussion, we focus on three broad approaches to design in HCI, first introduced in the opening chapter and revisited at the end of Chapter 3: engineering, science, and creative design. Many researchers and practitioners have speculated about the facets of HCI that fall into categories similar to these (e.g., Gold, 2007; Grudin, 2005; Harrison et al., 2007; Long and Dowell, 1989; McCrickard et al., 2004).

HCI has its roots in the engineering discipline. In reflecting on key objectives of engineering, primary concerns are with efficiency and reliability. Responding to the realistic needs of the interface development community, HCI practitioners with an engineering approach seek to build interfaces quickly and consistently in a way that will serve the desired process. Engineering as a discipline seeks procedures to operationalize best practices, allowing others to create usable interfaces and lending analytical structures to guide analysis within diverse contexts. Training HCI students to solve problems by using procedures and analytical methods supports and extends usability engineering practices.

HCI can also be viewed as a science. Some argue that interface designs are perfected over time, starting with observation that leads to hypotheses and testing, accumulating knowledge that eventually forms theory. Reducing interfaces to basic units that can be observed and tested in a variety of conditions provides laws that describe how these units interact, leading to new hypotheses and more constraints, rules, and exceptions to rules. The resulting network of requirements for observation and data collection is only valid with methods that enforce control and replication of results. As we grow as a scientific discipline, we can analyze new events and make reasonable hypotheses to predict their outcomes. HCI professionals should develop appreciation for this vision, as well as the tools to enact it.

HCI has elements of creative design. Creativity has long been valued in HCI, as researchers start with abstract patterns, then tailor them to the situation at hand. There is an art to balancing various constraints—embracing principles of design like contrast, opposition, and repetition, with the concerns of efficient information communication and user interaction. HCI professionals must value approaches that provide novel, satisfying, affective experiences.

Claims can be useful in engineering disciplines e.g., they can be combined with an approach like scenario-based design [Rosson and Carroll, 2002] to manage the growth and reuse of knowledge during design. As introduced in the first chapter, claims can be augmented such that they can be used more easily to index, categorize, and search for them, thus facilitating engineering processes. Section 4.1 outlines two engineering efforts that leveraged claims.

The hypothesis-based nature of claims make them a good match for the science behind design efforts. Essential to science is the ability to compare claims—to each other, or to metrics, or to some sort of figure of merit. Section 4.2 presents two studies that helped strengthen sets of claims.

Claims, like other approaches that can be categorized as design rationale, have been criticized as a hindrance to creative design—though appropriate scoping and presentation of design efforts has been argued to help foster creativity [Carroll, 2011]. It has been argued that claims can be a hindrance to creativity [Wahid et al., 2009], but one core element of claims—artifacts—has been argued to be important and useful during creative design, and particularly during ideation [Gaver and Martin, 2000; McCrickard et al., 2010]. As such, claims should be presented such that artifacts are visible during the growth of ideas, and the upsides and downsides and other parts of a claims are available during the pruning of ideas. Section 4.3 describes two ways to present claims in this way.

## 4.1   CLAIMS AND ENGINEERING

Engineering is perhaps the most foundational approach to HCI (at least for the ACM SIGCHI community), and many books and papers describe engineering approaches that leverage claims (e.g., Rosson and Carroll, 2002; Sutcliffe, 2002). This section presents two somewhat different engineering approaches, in which claims are central to the engineering process instead of peripheral. The first, adopted from Chewar et al. [2004b], looks at how claims augmented with critical parameter ratings can help drive the engineering of interfaces. The second, a case study described in detail in Lee et al. [2011], describes how a claims-based central design record can keep focus on a customer's needs during the engineering of an interface.

### 4.1.1   ENGINEERING INTERFACES WITH CRITICAL PARAMETERS

Engineers often face a difficult task in addressing unfamiliar problems that arise in engineering processes. We undertook this approach to explore how claims could be integrated into engineering processes with the help of *critical parameters*; cross-application terms focus on qualities that can be measured and reengineered to better serve the target user population [Newman, 1997]. Expressing new design problems in terms of critical parameter values allows efficient connection with theories and guidelines from psychology, sociology, and human factors—information that is otherwise difficult to obtain. Engineers are, in effect, using critical parameters as an index into a vast store of knowledge. However, this approach again relies on agreement with and consistency of critical parameters. In their current form, designers must know, understand, and accept the critical parameters of a field to benefit from them. The primary description of this research appears in a paper published at DIS 2004 [Chewar et al., 2004b] with an elaborated examination appearing in Christa Chewar's dissertation [Chewar, 2005]. The description in this chapter focuses on roles that critical parameters can play in claims-centered engineering processes.

Primary benefits of this approach may be found in helping engineers reflect on design tradeoffs and conduct mediated evaluation. improve the chance that these designers will be intrigued by HCI problems and develop innovative solutions. We are also hopeful that a critical parameter approach to interactive design research dialog can improve consensus of key issues, comparison of new efforts to existing efforts, and development of context-specific usability testing methods and instruments. As the community looks for approaches that will increase the likelihood of science of design, or support the practice of usability engineering, these arguments should be of interest, broadening as a topic of continued debate.

### Claims and critical parameters

Claims capture design knowledge that can be used in engineering efforts, but their most common forms do not provide easy ways to index, categorize, compare, and evaluate them. To address this issue, we looked to integrate critical parameters as an essential part of a claim. Critical parameters have three essential characteristics: their satisfaction is critical to the success of the system, they are persistent across successive systems, and must be manipulable by designers [Newman et al., 2000]. Newman presents arguments for adapting design practice with critical parameters, which others have extended as an approach for increasing cohesion and relevance within HCI research communities [Whittaker et al., 2000].

We augment critical parameters by associating with each a value between 0 and 1. Note that "0" does not equate to "bad" (or "1" to "good"); rather, it reflects a desired or measured level for the parameter. For example, for a critical parameter of "interruption", there are situations demanding a claim for which its desired level is very low (i.e., close to 0) when the designer wishes for the interface to promote continued primary task performance, but there are also situations demanding a claim for which its desired level is very high (i.e., approaching 1) to promote transition to a new, more important task.

Previous work proposed three critical parameters to capture user notification goals related to interruption, reaction, and comprehension (IRC) [McCrickard et al., 2003b]. Systems can be thought of as having targeted (design model) and actual (user's model) values for each parameter [Norman, 1986]. For example, a stock ticker notification system may be designed to target low interruption, low reaction, and high comprehension—but actual system usage may display a complete inversion of these parameters. Understanding targeted goals and user performance characteristics in terms that are comparable to each other and other systems provides opportunity for many benefits, but abstract parameters must be associated with concrete terms that can be assessed in usability engineering.

Three equations support notification systems interface engineering processes, allowing conversion of measurable, manageable concrete variables (conducted through previous work, available in McCrickard et al. [2003c]) to the abstract parameters that relate to general user goals and psychological effects. This is not intended to be a robust, exact system. Instead, the equations are intended as a conceptual metaphor, loosely organized as a categorical, interval scale approximation. When considering the validity of the equations, one should think of them as numeric representations of low, somewhat low, moderate, somewhat high, and high parameter categories. The equations are thought to assist in obtaining more consistent selection of these concrete categories while assigning abstract user's model parameter values. Numeric representations are useful in facilitating search/indexing operations. The full paper contains a case study (outlined in the next subsection) reflecting initial testing of this hypothesis [Chewar et al., 2004b]; a detailed example is provided in A.15.

*Interruption*   The first critical parameter for notification systems design is *interruption*. There have certainly been many important branches of work in cognitive and experimental psychology to understand the facets of interruption and to help identify claims that usability engineers can use as building blocks for future interface development [Bailey and Iqbal, 2008; Cutrell et al., 2001; Horvitz and Apacible, 2003; McCrickard et al., 2003a; McFarlane, 2002]. Seeking to improve this transfer of research findings, we offered a simplified model of interruption suitable for design and evaluation of notification systems:

$$I = 1 - s^{3 \times COI}$$

where $s$ = sustainment;
$COI$ = cost of interruption.

In this conception, interruption ($I$) can be described as the effect of reallocating attention from the primary task to the notification. "$I$" describes both the *appropriateness of an interruption*, as well as the *actual interruptive effect* of the notification artifact (distraction to the primary task). Therefore, "low $I$" can describe either an artifact that supports attention grading/parallel processing during the performance of an urgent primary task (high sustainment, regardless of $COI$) or any quality of multitasking performance in a non urgent situation (low $COI$, regardless of sustainment). *Appropriateness of an interruption* is represented by $COI$ (cost of interruption), characterizing the user's willingness to accept an interruption, and thus the urgency of the primary task can be inferred. As established by Horvitz's Interruption Workbench [Horvitz and Apacible, 2003], $COI$ describes a total task situation in terms of how much a given user would typically pay in dollars not to be interrupted based on data like the specific primary task application, level of ambient noise, recent keystroke and mouse activity, etc. *Actual interruptive effect(s)* can be gauged by primary task sustainment—a metric used to quantify the change in the primary task performance from solo-task to dual-task performance. Calculation of primary task sustainment has been demonstrated for notification interfaces [Tessendorf et al., 2002] and broader psychology efforts [Wickens and Hollands, 1999]; for example, if the primary task is editing a document, an evaluator can observe the solo-task performance characteristics related to a user's editing speed , accuracy, and thoroughness. The same performance characteristics can be compared in a dual-task situation (in which the notification system is also being monitored). Dividing the solo-task measures by the dual-task measures provides sustainment scores that can be averaged with weights that are appropriate to the situation context. This score provides an indication of the level of primary task performance that is typically sustained while a user is simultaneously monitoring or interacting with the notification system.

*Reaction*   The second abstract critical parameter term for notification systems, *reaction*, describes a user goal that can be generalized as an immediate response to a new notification:

$$R = \frac{(t \times h)^{\frac{1}{3 \times COI}}}{2} + \frac{h \times (0.5 + COI)}{3}$$

where $t$ = relative response time;
$h$ = hit rate.

The reaction ($R$) equation consists of two parts, each worth up to an $R$-value component of 0.5. The first term takes two reaction performance metrics—hit rate ($h$) and relative response time ($t$)—and lowers the average according to strength of $COI$. *Hit rate* refers to the concept from signal detection theory [Green and Swetz, 1966] where a user correctly detects and responds to a signal (a notification). *Relative response time* is a ratio between actual and expected response times. The second term of the $R$ equation can add up to half the hit rate to the $R$-value, depending on the strength of $COI$. Moderate reaction ($R$ =0.5) is scored when two-thirds of the hit rate and reaction time is achieved with a $COI$ of 0.5. Moderate or high $R$-values are always obtained when one of the variables is near maximum and the others are at least moderate.

The equation is also designed so that no more than $R$ =0.5 can be achieved if one of the three variables equals zero. To understand this rationale, one must consider that $R$ is a characterization of an artifact's effectiveness for supporting reaction in a dual-task situation. Both aspects of the reaction performance are also critical—a near-perfect hit rate would not be looked at as effective reaction if the response time were significantly slower than specification. Likewise, an acceptable response time has limited worth in the case that most signals delivered by the notification system are missed.

*Comprehension*   Comprehension is based on the concept of situation awareness [Endsley et al., 2003], in which a user accumulates Perception (of the elements in the system), Comprehension (of the current situation), and then Projection (of future status). Each level is dependent on achieving some part of the preceding level, and represents a progressively higher state of situated awareness. Thinking of notification comprehension as situation awareness leverages research in the human factors field and reinforces the argument that each parameter is a separable dimension. For instance, studies have shown that we can recognize the characteristics of awareness independent of the processes required to maintain it (working and long-term memory or attentional state) [Adams et al., 1995] or the response selections that result from it [Whittaker et al., 2000]. Thus, the comprehension critical parameter describes longer-term (not immediate) knowledge gain:

$$C = \frac{p + (1 - p)(c + f(1 - c))}{3} + \frac{c + f(1 - c)}{3} + \frac{f}{3}$$

where $p$ = perception rate,

$c$ = base comprehension,

$f$ = projection (future).

The three portions of the equation, added together, correspond to the three levels of situation awareness: perception, base comprehension, and projection. Each level can contribute up to a third of the total $C$ value. *Perception* reflects the notification system's support for invoking signal hits rather than false alarms. *Base comprehension* reflects a user's ability to interpret and remember information displayed in the system. *Projection* reflects the user's ability to make inferences about the displayed information (e.g., likely changes over time). All together, comprehension describes the extent to which a notification system imparts (and is expected to impact) understanding of new information based on the actions taken by the user, cued recollection of states and trends, and accuracy of inferences based on the notification information. Certainly, an evaluator must make these judgements based on information that is inherently part of the task context; thus creating a close dependence on the situation and context in which the claim will be used. However, the comprehension equation seeks to provide a structure to map this specific, task-related assessment for use in a more generic claim that can be used and reused more broadly.

*Intended use*   These equations represent a conceptual metaphor to connect concrete critical parameter terms with abstract terms that can be generalized to understand design spaces—toward creating a claims-based engineering process to support design knowledge reuse and compare interfaces within a common design domain. Each variable on the right side of an equation is a concrete term that can be measured in requirements gathering and usability testing with empirical or analytical methods. Empirical methods could include system event logging, user observation, and user surveys; analytical methods could include surveys of experts, cognitive walkthroughs, or the use of a tool like Horvitz's Interruption Workbench [Horvitz and Apacible, 2003] (as seen previously in the calculation of COI). An engineer must balance the cost of employing the method with its expected benefit in determining the appropriate method for each claim.

Abstract and concrete terms for critical parameters like these can be introduced for any other class of interactive system (e.g., in-vehicle navigation, informational kiosks) to describe user goals and psychological effects of the interface. Associating critical parameters with claims can connect a design community and support common design efforts toward measurably better products. The critical parameters also can be used as an indexing mechanism for claims repositories, allowing designers to compare claims with similar parameter ratings. While there are certainly other factors that contribute to the quality of a design effort (see McCrickard and Chewar, 2003), the use of critical parameters can provide an important tool to support engineering processes.

**Case study examples: Scope redesign**

To exercise the use of critical parameters associated with claims, a group of novice designers were challenged to improve upon a notification system interface developed by Microsoft Research [van Dantzich et al., 2002]. Scope (shown in Figure 4.1) is a small display that resides in the corner of a user's desktop, depicting new and existing notifications in quadrants for email, calendar, task, and alert items. As a circular-shaped interface, the Scope leverages a radar metaphor to convey relative item urgency. In their research, the original design group noted several usability concerns, so we instructed the new teams (15 total) to improve upon these and other issues they discovered through their own requirements gathering efforts. The three-month redesign effort was controlled through class specifications that required a mediated approach to advancing design rationale and making interface improvements.

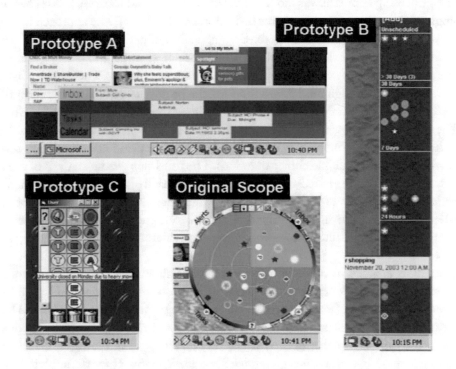

**Figure 4.1:** Notification systems interfaces studied in the case study usability evaluation (from McCrickard et al., 2003b).

Motivated by their requirements gathering results rather than specific instructions, several of the teams abandoned the radar metaphor claims to establish very different display and interaction claims for the Scope redesign. We selected three interface redesigns (see Figure 4.1) for analysis: Prototype A uses a bulletin board metaphor, with notifications appearing as notes in categorical rows; Prototype B employs a waterfall metaphor, where notification icons fall slowly down as they near their due date; Prototype C uses an icon-based task list that can be reordered and coded by urgency. We assumed that the described metaphors would be the dominant factor in the evaluation, as all designs otherwise included similar features.

We wanted to compare redesign options according to impact on notification critical parameters, positioning each interface within the design space that is defined by the critical parameters. We expected that quantifying the conceptual models would help to identify the interface claims best suited for redesign in subsequent versions, to suggest additional necessary design and requirement gathering steps, and to classify claims for design and reuse. The remainder of this section provides an overview of our approach and results; a more complete description can be found in Chewar et al. [2004b] and Chewar [2005].

Our engineering approach was modified from the Rosson and Carroll's [2002] scenario-based usability engineering, with a focus on claims definition and validation. The approach leverages Norman's concept of a design model (the targeted designers' view of how the system should behave) and a user's model (an actual user view reflecting system behavior)—seeking to create a user model that matches the design model, as measured by IRC critical parameter values. The first step in our testing procedure was to collect design model intention for the prototype designs in the form of targeted IRC values from each system's design team, using a designer tool validated previously [Chewar et al., 2004b]. The second step engaged 11 or 12 experienced designers in 20- to 35-min moderated analytical evaluations of the prototype systems, highlighted by a demo and discussion session then concluded with a series of multiple choice questions. The third step was an analysis of the data from the expert design, resulting in an IRC user's model values for each of the systems. Fourth, we checked each collection of IRC values to eliminate variance (when there were a small number of outliers) or create clusters (when multiple distinct evaluation values became apparent). Finally, we examined the data to determine that the evaluation approach helped evaluators achieve consistency within each prototype.

Our analysis enabled us to make recommendations about each prototype (pictured in Figure 4.1). Prototype A had a design model targeting moderately low interruption ($I = .39$, on a scale of 0 to 1), moderate reaction ($R = .46$), and moderately high comprehension ($C = .61$). However, one cluster of evaluators reflected that both interruption and reaction would be moderately low ($I = .36, R = .35$) and comprehension would be very low ($C = .18$). However, the second cluster agreed much more closely with the design model: $I = .35, R = .54, C = .62$, implying that the design may meet intentions for some users or in certain situations. Mitigating the concerns expressed by evaluators in the first cluster would be an important next step for these designers, perhaps by addressing evaluator concerns involving clutter, overlap, and poor scalability. Another issue raised was a potential user inability to ascertain relative urgency of notifications—a feature apparent in the original Scope that enhances reaction.

Prototype B design models were much less consistent across the design team—reflecting dissention or disagreement among team members—but on average reflected moderately high values for interruption and comprehension ($I = .61, C = .63$) and moderate reaction values ($R = .57$). Evaluators consistently rated this system with moderately low interruption and reaction ($I = .26, R = .27$) and moderately high comprehension ($C = .66$). As might be expected, the designer team was displeased with the evaluation result. In this case, the critical parameter models reveal a need for renegotiation of the requirement assumptions for the basic user goals. This process can be assisted by discussing specific points on the design model survey.

The prototype C design model consistently targeted moderate interruption ($I = .48$) and moderately high reaction and comprehension ($R = .71, C = .67$). According to both clusters of evaluators, the prototype did not match the design model. Both clusters agreed that reaction would be moderately low ($R = .24$ and $.21$), a major difference from the design model that would be essential to correct. Evaluators were concerned that new notifications would be detected too slowly, since user memory overhead would be too high without any glanceable notification context and the interface's scrolling mechanism would be problematic. One cluster saw these problems as a basis for moderately high interruption ($I = .79$), while the other cluster felt the interface would simply be ignored and introduce interruption less than intended ($I = .29$). Both clusters thought only moderate comprehension gains would be supported by this interface ($C = .57$ and $.45$). Faced with these large disparities, the design team may be wise to consider an alternate approach.

While the IRC parameters were useful in assessing each design individually, the broader benefits of using critical parameters are recognized in activities such as system comparison and design knowledge reuse. For example, if we are looking for a more ambient redesign of the Scope, Prototype B would be the best starting point. However, techniques used in Prototype A may offer relevant inspiration, and it may be wise to conduct an evaluation on the Scope to see whether real critical parameter improvements are even being proposed. As information and interaction design changes are made to any system, a series of IRC evaluations can show progress between versions, as well as specific effects of feature-level artifacts. These psychological effects can be recorded as claims that are indexed by their IRC values and archived in a library for design knowledge reuse. For engineers that seek to create targeted design models that are measurably better than current options—through the creation of new artifacts, the use of novel metaphors, or the leveraging of existing claims—such a library may be an indispensable resource.

## 4.1.2    ENGINEERING INTERFACES USING AGILE METHODS

Agile software development methodologies have emerged as an efficient and effective way in software engineering to address many of the risks in developing software—such as changing requirements, slipping development schedules and cost overruns—by using practices like incremental test-driven development and leveraging onsite customers. However, agile methods traditionally did not originally incorporate practices from usability engineering. As a result, agile teams would often develop systems that were difficult to use, and practitioners and researchers have been exploring ways to integrate usability into agile software development methodologies [Patton, 2002]. Our contributions to these efforts has considered how claims, scenarios, and other engineering tools and methods can help address many of the tension points between agility and usability through an approach we call eXtreme Scenario-based Design (XSBD). This research was spearheaded by Jason Chong Lee, in cooperation with a local company, Meridium, and more complete accountings of this work appear elsewhere [Lee et al., 2011; Lee and McCrickard, 2007; Lee et al., 2008]. This section focuses on the contribution that claims make to the XSBD engineering process, including examples of it in practice. An example claim from the Lee XSBD work is in A.17.

### Claims and agile usability

The XSBD process draws on concepts from usability engineering and agile software development. In the XSBD process, the same core steps of scenario-based design (SBD)—requirements analysis, activity design, and information and interaction design—are followed [Rosson and Carroll, 2002]. However, they proceed in concert with software development. This parallel approach is common in agile usability methods (e.g., Fox et al., 2008). This allows potentially time-consuming and non-interdependent processes to occur in parallel. The XSBD approach assumes that an experienced usability engineer is a member of team and is working with the developers to implement the system.

To accentuate the user experience with design representations and to help ensure that the user interface meets the needs of the end users and customer, we created the Central Design Record (CDR). The CDR is an extension of Norman's system image, adapted for use in agile scenario-based design [Norman, 1986]. It allows the usability engineer to work within the incremental agile development cycle while maintaining the high-level vision of the interface. It helps the usability engineer to execute usability evaluations that fit within the agile framework while validating that the user interface is usable and meets the high-level goals of the system. Finally, it supports communication of design rationale to other XSBD team members and helps them make more balanced design decisions. The CDR is primarily managed by a usability engineer (or a team of usability engineers) with input from the rest of the team.

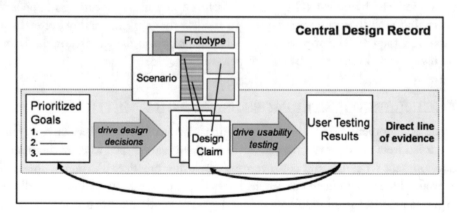

**Figure 4.2:** The main elements and interconnections in the Central Design Record (CDR) (from Lee et al., 2008).

The CDR (see Figure 4.2 and Appendix A.17) uses prioritized project goals to drive design decisions that are captured in claims. The claims capture design decisions, supported by scenarios and exemplified by prototypes. XSBD *claims* are similar to agile design *stories* in that they are brief descriptions of system features, but claims are used by the usability engineer in XSBD to capture and guide design decisions rather than to aid in project planning and management. *Scenarios*, which are used in a traditional SBD sense to describe common workflows in a narrative form, are used in conjunction with mockups to give developers an end-to-end understanding of how the system will be used. While agile *stories* might seem like a close match conceptually to SBD's *scenarios*, we found that stories are actually more like claims in their size and purpose—and as such they are used to drive the dialog and decision-making during design sessions. *Prototypes* typically come in the form of mockups that encapsulate the meaning of one or more claims and have emerged as one of the primary mechanisms the usability engineer uses to communicate the UI design to developers.

XSBD has two separate but synchronized usability and development tracks, with regular meetings (every one to four weeks) to hand off designs and reach consensus on design decisions. The usability engineering team works one iteration ahead of the developers so designs can be handed off for developers to start implementing those designs in the following iteration. These parallel tracks, common in other agile usability approaches (e.g., Fox et al., 2008), allow the team to optimize its velocity while still developing a system that meets high-level design goals. Using this handoff system, the two tracks can work largely in parallel, with the regular meetings driving decisions about usability testing (see Figure 4.2); in fact, they drive all usability engineering decisions that are made—whether they be lab-based testing decisions, expert review, further claims development, prototyping, or other decisions.

XSBD has been used in usability engineering sessions both in academia [Lee and McCrickard, 2007] and industry [Lee et al., 2011, 2008] for both distributed and co-located design teams. The next subsection describes some of the claims-related lessons extracted from this work (and described more fully in the cited publications). While each of these efforts were rooted in engineering approaches, we highlight instances where claims facilitate crossover to science and design approaches.

**Case study examples: mobile interface creation**

This section draws from two XSBD projects that were joint efforts between Virginia Tech and Meridium, Inc. One was the development of a touch screen application to replace and improve a paper-based work order system [Lee et al., 2008]. This project engaged a co-located team including a project lead, a product lead, two developers, a quality assurance person, and a usability engineer. The other project was a distributed web development effort, with two managers, a testing lead, a development lead, a documentation person and a usability engineer at one site and the core development and testing team at another site [Lee et al., 2011]. Many of the issues from that project stemmed from the difference in location among team members.

In both instances of XSBD application in the workplace, details about the project are proprietary. As such, this section highlights usability-related points of interest within the engineering efforts without in-depth discussion regarding the context or specific results.

*Balancing design decisions*    Claims proved to be a useful way to capture design decisions and address conflicting opinions in the touch screen project. For example, one of the claims that looked at popup warnings balanced upsides regarding gaining user attention, providing relevant information, and avoiding frustration with their flashy and sometimes disorienting nature. But the usability engineer gave positive feedback about the claims: "They helped me keep focus and overall they helped me get the evidence I needed to open up discussions with teammates about the interface".

Claims allowed the usability engineer to provide other team members with rationale for design features and describe why they were important. They provided a platform for discussion about features and their role in the system. This helped in prioritizing the backlog of features that were planned for subsequent iterations.

In addition, since the user interface is the most visible portion of system under development, team members often gave their own opinions about how the interface should be designed based on their own past experiences and knowledge of similar systems. Many times, this sort of feedback was valuable. However, this sometimes resulted in tensions between the usability engineer and developers about how the system should be designed. Claims were used to resolve these kinds of disagreements. If another team member proposed a change to a system feature as designed by the usability engineer, the usability engineer would record the suggestion in the form of a claim. Typically, the original design of the usability engineer would be used initially and would be evaluated. If a problem was uncovered, the proposed change would then be considered.

*Project startup difficulties*   Early on in the distributed project, the usability engineer had trouble working ahead of developers. The usability engineer was brought on board during the first iteration after the developers had already started developing the user interface. This resulted in designs that did not meet high-level design goals. In addition, the offsite developers were reluctant to rework what they had already done. Developers would come up with designs without consideration for target users and usability goals. This may have continued because the usability engineer was working part-time on the team. She was not present at all daily meetings and hence was not able to immediately answer questions that developers and other team members had. The quality assurance manager noted the negative impact from confusion and rework.

Linking goals in the CDR to the claims and other features enabled the usability engineer to catch up. She had to first evaluate the existing implemented UI. She then quickly defined design goals, user description, claims, and other aspects of the CDR as she worked to design for the next iteration to get ahead of the developers. The usability engineer focused on only the most critical features of the system as defined by the goals. She generated claims to capture key tradeoffs of specific features that directly related to the high-level goals of the system.

*Collaboration issues*   Collaboration issues arose in the touch screen project as a result of interactions between the developers and the usability engineer—often centered upon a lack of prior experience working with a usability engineer among members of the development team and an imbalance in time spent (and quantity of work accomplished) by the part-time usability engineer and the multiple full-time developers. The offsite developers would proceed with designs with direct impact on interface usability without input from the usability engineer, then would be reluctant to rework what they had already done. The quality assurance manager noted that: "This has a negative impact because it causes lots of confusion and dev and testing rework".

The team chose to have increased focus on using the CDR to link goals to evaluated design features to prioritize usability work only on the most important features of the system. The usability engineer had to first evaluate the existing implemented UI. She then quickly defined design goals, user description, claims, and other aspects of the CDR as she worked to design for the next iteration to get ahead of the developers. The usability engineer focused on only the most critical features of the system as defined by the goals. She generated claims to capture key tradeoffs of specific features that directly related to the high level goals of the system.

For example, to respond to the goal of making the system easy for novices, the usability engineer crafted a claim that balanced upsides and downsides for removing the "hide record explorer" task bar. While all agreed that the ability to hide the task bar would save space (upside), there were no cognitive clues of its use and it was not consistent with other expand/collapse features (downside). A usability test confirmed that users were unable to hide the task bar, and, more importantly, could not figure out how to open it once it was hidden. Lightweight evaluations such as this were typically run in a single day with a small group of participants at Meridium who had similar characteristics with the end users of the system. Non-critical features were typically designed and implemented by the offsite developers and signed off on by the usability engineer after she reviewed them at the iteration review meetings.

By using the CDR to focus on only the most important features of the system, the usability engineer was able to sync up with the developers by the third iteration, and she begin delivering feature designs and redesign requests to them to implement in the subsequent iteration. Being able to share and communicate the reasoning behind decisions based on goals, design claims, and testing results helped the usability engineer better show the rest of the team why they were being made and why they were important.

*Distributed teams*    Since the web development teams were distributed and working asynchronously, sharing and maintaining up-to-date documents, artifacts, and claims was challenging. These problems were addressed by introducing a more structured, regimented information sharing process then one might find in a collocated agile team. For example, at an early daily meeting, the problem of sharing design information between distributed team members was brought up. The project team used email to share documents, and as a result the documents were getting out of sync: the usability engineer would send out a version of the design for the upcoming iteration and then later would send out an updated version, but one of the offsite developers might accidentally implement the older design. The distributed nature of the team magnified these issues as the team could not communicate synchronously and the problem might not surface until the iteration review meeting. In addition, if the usability engineer or other team members missed a meeting it was difficult to get synced up. This was somewhat common as the daily meetings occurred near the beginning of the day for the onsite members and at the end of the day for the offsite members. As one developer noted: "There is no way for the developers to convey the details about what is being delivered…to team members who didn't attend the meeting. If someone did not attend one meeting, they will not know what exactly is functional and what is yet to be delivered in a feature".

The team clearly defined the mechanisms through which the usability engineer would deliver designs and how the team would communicate design issues as they arose. The usability engineer would meet at the beginning of each iteration with the product manager to validate the design to be implemented in the next iteration. The usability engineer then uploaded that design to the online team portal by the end of the day. When possible, the offshore developers would demo implemented functionality during the daily meetings so the usability engineer could compare against the designs and also so any small issues the developers had with the design could be addressed. Any other questions or issues that the developers encountered were addressed by posting those issues in the online discussion board. The issues were then reviewed at the start of each daily meeting.

If the usability engineer saw any major discrepancies between the design and the implementation or if the team has some specific concerns about a design feature, she would document them in the form of claims—utilizing claims not only as a brainstorming and idea unification tool but as a central aspect of knowledge capture and documentation. These claims would then either be tested later by the usability engineer or otherwise resolved through by consensus of the team. The project had to trade off improved information sharing within the team at the cost of increased documentation and process structure. The structured process and tools the team used to collaborate and share information may seem counter to the agile principle of valuing "individuals and interactions over processes and tools" [Lee et al., 2008] at first glance. Although the team had to document more information and share it in a more structured way, it improved the way that the distributed team members were interacting and communicating with each other. This compromise minimized the amount of additional documentation and allowed the offsite development team to make quick fixes when needed. It also reduced confusions and misunderstandings, as the team was previously not using a unified way to track such changes to the system.

Overall, we found that the adoption of the XSBD approach was hampered by the distributed nature of the team since the effective use of the approach depends on consistent and regular communication between team members. In particular, the team did not adopt and use claims as extensively in a distributed group [Lee et al., 2011] as when the XSBD approach was used by a collocated team [Lee et al., 2008]. As we noted in Chapter 2 with the use of Compendium in co-located groups, the act of constructing a claim with others watching and contributing contains a social component that is difficult to overcome in distributed setting.

## 4.2   CLAIMS AND SCIENCE

Claims were first introduced as "falsifiable hypotheses", both in its formal definition as part of argumentation and rhetoric [Toulmin, 1958] and in its introduction to HCI [Carroll and Kellogg, 1989]. However, it seems that claims have been used as more of a gateway to an engineering or creative design process—an early brainstorming technique or a scenario analysis tool rather than a conduit for good science. This section explores two experiments that drew their focus from the analysis and comparison of claims: the first an examination of effective speech for notifications (detailed in Bhatia and McCrickard, 2006); the second a comparison of gesture and touch (drawn from Karam et al., 2009). In both examples, claims were used by select members of the team to narrow down the focus of the experiments to interesting questions and to revisit the contribution of the experiments upon their completion.

## 4.2.1    A SCIENTIFIC APPROACH TO UNDERSTANDING AUDITORY NOTIFICATIONS

Claims served as guideposts during our investigation into the roles of different voice types in notifications [Bhatia and McCrickard, 2006]. Our investigation was rooted in the work of Gaver and his colleagues [Gaver et al., 1991], in which they established "an ecology of auditory icons" to convey information in multitasking situations (specifically, in a factory environment). They explored the effects of familiar and unfamiliar sounds of simulated machines to allow users to determine whether a machine was working correctly, incorrectly, or not at all. An observation of eight pairs of participants revealed benefit in using familiar sounds, packaged as "auditory icons", to understand occurrences, affect collaboration, and support division of labor—all while more freely moving around the physical space.

These claims built on knowledge gleaned from the Gaver work and follow-up efforts (e.g., Nass and Gong, 2000; Sawhney et al., 1999), we considered whether familiarity of voices might have similar effects in dynamic group situations. We sought to identify statistically significant differences in voices for notification situations. A scientific approach to design and statistical significance of results (not a concern for Gaver in his efforts) were important to us, so we leveraged the work of Gaver and others in constructing claims, vetting them in larger group meetings to ascertain which claims were most important to consider because of potential interest to systems designers and because of a lack of support in prior research and design efforts.

As with the engineering efforts described in the previous section, we were guided by a desire to understand three critical parameters: interruption, reaction, and comprehension. Based on Gaver's work, we framed our approach in terms of *claims* that a familiar voice would lead to faster reaction for an individual and greater comprehension among a group, while an unfamiliar voice would lead to increased interruption. However, the evidence in support of the claims (both the upsides and the downsides) is weak, given that Gaver considered a different domain and did not seek to attain statistically significant results. (In fact, Nass listed the effect of voice familiarity on information processing as an open question in Nass and Gong, 2000.) As such, we sought to define a way to measure interruption, reaction, and comprehension for voice notifications and to capture results through a user study.

Interruption was measured by the drop in game performance, determined by comparing the percentage of blocks caught before and after the voice notification. The change in catch rate was used as an indicator of the interruption caused by the voice. To measure reaction, participants were asked to hit the space bar as soon as they heard the voice notification. The time difference between the start of voice notification and the user hitting the space bar is reaction time measured in milliseconds. Correctness in remembering the numbers, entered at the end of the game, was used to calculate the comprehension parameter. Due to practical constraints, only this fairly short-term recall value was measured for comprehension.

Twenty-seven volunteers participated in this experiment. Participants were recruited from an undergraduate class and were given the incentive of extra credit for taking part in the experiment. The experiment was conducted in a quiet computer lab, with each participant wearing a headset to hear the audio. Each session lasted approximately 30 min. Participants were required to first record the numbers 0–9 in their own voice. Each number was recorded in a span of 1 s so that there would be uniformity in the way the numbers were read out. The class instructor volunteered to serve as the familiar voice. For the unfamiliar voice, we chose the voice of a person that none of the participants were familiar with—an individual with a French accent (we verified that none of the participants had ever regularly been exposed to a French accent). Since the class instructor's voice would not be as familiar as that of a friend or a co-worker, the choice of an accented voice to broaden the difference between familiar and unfamiliar seems reasonable.

Before starting the experiment, the users were asked a series of questions to help us assess their different cultural and social backgrounds. Users were then given four practice rounds to familiarize themselves with the game and environment. The experiment itself consisted of nine rounds. During each round, the game was interrupted by a voice reading out a seven-digit number (the same length as a phone number). The users had to hit the space bar upon hearing the notification, then remember the numbers as they continued playing the game and enter them into a box at the end of the round. The users heard a different voice in each round. A Latin square design was used to control variation among the three voice types, with each user assigned to one of three groups in which the users heard each voice three times in different orders. Each round lasted for one minute, with voice notification approximately 25 s into the game and lasting for approximately 7 s.

ANOVA test results suggested that there is a significant difference in the means for the reaction time among the three voices ($F(2,215)=3.74$, MSE=48785.42, $p=0.025$). The mean reaction time to the user's own voice (M=831.83, SD=213.92) was significantly faster than the familiar voice (M=915.62, SD=225.8), $t(143)=-2.29$, $p=0.023$. User's own voice was also significantly faster compared to the unfamiliar voice (M=921.31, SD=222.78), $t(144)=-2.47$, $p=0.014$. The t-test between familiar and unfamiliar voice did not reveal any significant differences. Thus, participants reacted most quickly to their own voice.

The slower reaction time for the unfamiliar voice corresponds with the idea that we tend to filter out voices of people we do not know. The quickest reaction time to one's own voice came as a surprise. Listening to one's own voice might have evoked an emotional response that relates to a self-image. This in turn may have triggered the fast reaction time that showed that you are acknowledging yourself. It must also be noted that the instructor's voice was not an extremely familiar voice for the student participants. The students had only been exposed to it in a classroom setting for about thirty hours. Our supposition is that increased familiarity with a voice will lead to similar reaction times to one's own voice; that is, very familiar voices like those of close friends, co-workers, roommates, etc., will have characteristics similar to that of your own voice.

An ANOVA test showed near significant difference for interruption for the three voices $F(2,173)=2.33$, MSE$=5.476$, p$=0.099$. This motivated t-tests, with the t-test between one's own voice and the unfamiliar voice, revealed a significant difference between performance before and after the notification, with performance calculated by the percentage of balls caught from the total number of balls. The mean reduction in catch rate was significantly larger for the own voice condition (M$=4.06$, SD$=2.64$) than with the unfamiliar voice (M$=3.11$, SD$=2.08$), $t(112)=2.11$, p$=0.036$. Therefore, one's own voice has a higher interruption level than the unfamiliar voice. The high interruption possibly occurs for the same reason as the high reaction for your own voice. While further study is needed to explore the validity of this result, this initial finding is encouraging.

Recall was consistently high for all three voice types (Own M$=6.76$, SD$=0.50$; Familiar M$=6.65$, SD$=0.69$; Unfamiliar M$=6.74$, SD$=0.54$ for numbers recalled correctly out of 7 numbers), with no statistically significant results to report. The consistently high recall, combined with a cognitively demanding primary task, suggests that voice in general should support adequate short-term recall for many situations.

The results from this short-term study strengthened our belief in certain aspects of the claims, though our desire for broader confirmation demanded that we examine the voice notifications through a long-term study. Bhatia and McCrickard [2006] present analysis from a two-month deployment of Notiframe, a voice notification system to notify people about the start and end time for meetings. It used an audio clip with the voice of the person who scheduled the meeting to signal meeting times—seeking to validate our claim that people's attention will be drawn by a familiar voice. Results tended to strengthen aspects of the claims with regard to familiar voices—people tended to recognize them and engage with each other in early discussions in preparation for the meetings. But unfamiliar voices tended to lead to much higher interruption, as people in the lab tried to guess to whom the voice belonged. The downsides regarding unfamiliar voices on Notiframe outweighed the upsides gained from messages from familiar voices, and the Notiframe interface was not used beyond the two-month study period.

## 4.2.2   A SCIENTIFIC APPROACH TO COMPARING GESTURE AND TOUCH

Touch-based interaction for large displays has been a focus for research for many years, but in situations where minimal interruption is important, gestures have potential for improved performance. Our research group took part in a project led by visiting scholar Maria Karam that investigated relative performance of touch and gesture responses to notifications using a claims-based approach to the IRC framework [Karam et al., 2009]. Karam was drawn to our work on claims and critical parameters, using them to guide her research efforts on gesture notifications. Together, we wanted to use claims and critical parameters to understand when and whether semaphoric gestures (those from a specific alphabet of gestures) could support improved behavior when compared to touch interactions. The lead author was only on site for a few days to plan the research effort, so it was vital to work as efficiently as possible in a focused manner—but it was important that everyone's areas of expertise be represented in the planning of the paper.

Early-stage brainstorming using claims—together with the expanded set of notification critical parameters of interruption, reaction, comprehension, and satisfaction found in McCrickard et al. [2003b]—was used to identify potential areas to study experimentally. The questions that arose from an initial email exchange and on-site meetings about target critical parameters led to a multi-part claim about semaphoric gestures, listed here (with IRC+S terms highlighted).

---

**responding to a notification using a semaphoric gesture**

+ results in less *interruptive* interactions than touch screen interactions

+ support more efficient *reaction* to both high and low interruption notifications

+ are as intuitive, easy, and efficient to use (*satisfaction*) as touch-screens for interacting with notifications

− BUT are no better at supporting *comprehension* levels of the content on the notifications

---

To measure interruption, our thought was to observe whether there was higher primary task performance with the gesture interactions. Reaction would be measured by considering secondary task performance times. Comprehension would be defined by success rates for secondary tasks completed. And higher satisfaction corresponds to higher subjective ratings and user preference. Certainly each of the critical parameters can be explored in much greater detail through an expanded definition/consideration of the constituent parts. But we felt this effort would represent an important advance in the current state-of-the-knowledge.

To test the effectiveness of using gestures as an input modality for notification system interactions, we created a dual-task situation that simulated a command and control environment requiring users to monitor and interact with multiple information systems simultaneously. The primary task required participants to search through a satellite photo, and locate a specific area on the satellite within a specified time limit. The satellite image was displayed at a resolution of $1024 \times 768$ on a 136 cm $\times$ 101 cm SmartBoard large touch screen as the primary display. Users had to locate the target area within the satellite image, which was displayed on the right side of the screen as a $45 \times 45$ pixel. For the secondary task, participants monitored a notification system animation presented on a peripheral secondary display located to the side of the primary display. (See the setup in Figure 4.3.)

We simulated user interactions on the peripheral display, providing two levels of interruption: low and high. The wizard used a wireless keyboard to control the peripheral display input in response to participant actions (gestures or touch). Both the gestures and touch interactions were simulated by the wizard during the experiment to further control for differences in the two systems and to reduce the confounds arising from user variation in experience and in learning to use these two input

**Figure 4.3:** Setup for the gesture/touchscreen experiment (from Karam et al., 2009).

techniques. Participants performed single right-handed gestures and touch input for the secondary task, which was located to the right of the SmartBoard but were free to use either hand to select regions on the main display and resume the primary task. We recruited 20 undergraduate and graduate students from a variety of disciplines at Virginia Tech to participate in the study.

The experiment was a full factorial, repeated measures design with interaction modes (gesture and touch) as the within-participant factor, and the interruption level (high or low) as the between-participant factor. The interaction modes were counter-balanced within participants, consisting of one set of trials using gestures, and the other using a touch screen. For the low interruption condition, a visual notification was used, and in the high interruption condition, both an audio and visual notification were presented to the participants. We tested four conditions, and they are coded based on the interruption level of the notification (0= low, 1= high) and counterbalancing (G= gestures seen first, T=Touch screen seen first). The four conditions were thus 0G (low interruption, gestures first), 0T (low interruption, touch first), 1G (high interruption, gestures first), and 1T (high interruption, gestures first). Our within-participant variable was the interaction mode, where each participant used both the touch screen and the gesture interaction. The between-participant variable used in the experiment consisted of altering the interruption level so that in the low interruption condition, participants only received a visual notification for the secondary task, and in the high interruption condition, participants received both an audio and the visual notifications.

To investigate different settings of the IRC values for notification system interactions, we created two interaction contexts to compare gesture and touch input for supporting effective notification system interactions. To determine the degree of interruption and efficiency of semaphoric gesture vs. touch screen, we measured reaction time, recovery time, and secondary task time. Times when a notification was issued and when the primary task resumed were recorded by software. The time of the response to the notification was logged via keypress at the wizard's station. Regarding the relative ease of execution of gesture vs. touch, we looked for significant differences in reaction and recovery times. To infer effects on attention, we calculated the search success rates and measured the search times (primary task). We also recorded the number of secondary tasks completed and the total time to perform each (secondary task time).

Analysis was conducted using ANOVA/MANOVA testing, combined with subjective ratings from the participants. Full results reported in Karam et al. [2009]. Revisiting the claim that helped define the directions of the paper, we consider how the upsides and downsides are influenced by the study results:

**responding to a notification using a semaphoric gesture**

+ results in less *interruptive* interactions than touch screen interactions

+ support more efficient *reaction* to both high and low interruption notifications

+ are as intuitive, easy, and efficient to use (*satisfaction*) as touch-screens for interacting with notifications

− BUT are no better at supporting *comprehension* levels of the content on the notifications

Results from this study suggest that gestures were less interruptive than touch for interacting with notification systems for non-critical secondary tasks. While our results show that the significant differences in performance are primarily affected by condition rather than the interaction modes, we observe that semaphoric gestures support less interruptive interactions with notification systems than touch-based interactions for low interruption secondary tasks. While this strengthens the first claim upside, it also may require a rewording of the upside to address the particular observed condition (non-critical secondary tasks) or a pointer within the upside to the paper describing the experiment.

Experiment results show that reaction time in the gesture condition does not significantly differ from the touch screen condition—providing no strength to the second claim upside. Since our interaction scenario used similar interaction zones for both gestures and touch, we observe that the increased interaction zone possible with gestures would thus be more effective in a pervasive or ubiquitous computing environment where interactions at a distance are required. The expert opinions that led to this upside still provide some strength for it, but further study is required to more fully confirm or refute the upside.

Our metrics for satisfaction reflected a preference for gesture interactions. Most participants experienced gestures as a less disruptive interaction, and it permitted easier resumption of their primary task. For gestures, several users reported an ability to search without feeling tied to the secondary display. The benefit of gesturing in-place avoids re-purposing one's hands to carry out a secondary task such as responding to a notification, and avoids changing ones physical position such that the current context in the focal search task is lost. Thus, after a period of adjustment, gesturing was seen as easier by the majority of participants.

Results also support the claim downside, as secondary task completion rates or comprehension levels seemed unaffected by input mode. Rather, familiarity with the tasks and the interruption level of the notification played a more significant role. This result points to possibilities for other claims relating to task familiarity and to connections between interruption level and comprehension.

Our results show the most benefit for gesture occurs when attention draw is low. The benefit appeared to be masked in the high interruption group, as there was no significant difference in performance. We note that the higher interruption was an increased rate of visual strobe with an accompanying sound; as expected, this was sufficient to reduce the reaction times. However, the greater level of distraction meant that participants lost the benefit of gesture over touch-screen interaction. We provided a spatially appropriate cue, which caused eye gaze to be diverted to the notification task. This effect interfered with the eyes-free benefit of gestures—suggesting areas in which the claim could be applied successfully, and areas in which further investigation is needed.

## 4.3    CLAIMS AND DESIGN

The term *design* is used by all fields, but in recent years it has come to refer to the craft-related activity viewed as distinct from science and engineering—rooted in art, craft, and architecture, with creativity as a central tenet. While design and creativity can focus on the creative product [Amabile, 1982; Boden, 1994] or the creative person [Guilford, 1950], this section considers the creative process; specifically, how to enhance creative endeavors, and how to support creativity in HCI-focused design processes.

This section looks at two explorations of the creative process. The first, from an unpublished reflection on a map of claims taken from a project near completion, asks project participants to reflect upon the designs and consider alternative or future paths. It was our expectation that a visual overview, with much of the detailed information provided as a secondary resource, would inspire creative ideas. But, despite a few notable successes, even by hiding the upsides and downsides, this approach seemed too constraining in the type of comments that it elicited. The second exploration (elaborated in a series of papers, McCrickard et al., 2011; Wahid et al., 2009, 2010, 2011) looks not at a graph-based representation of a claim set late in design, but at picture-based representations of the individual claims early in design. Again, most of the rationale was hidden, and participants were encouraged to create their own representations through grouping and storyboarding—but with this representation of claims, there were many more instances in which the participants were provoked toward creative ideas.

### 4.3.1  CLAIMS MAPS

Claims maps capture relationships among sets of claims to capture the rationale that guided a design or to demonstrate possible connections among sets of claims. This section describes several instances of claims maps in the literature, and it provides a yet-unpublished case study of the use of claims maps in understanding the design of a bug tracker visualization interface created at IBM.

The first conceptualization of claims maps appeared in Singley and Carroll [1996] in which they demonstrate how a claims map can "provide rationale for the current state of the design, but also [summarize] the design history". Claims maps visually represent claims as nodes, with links showing a "responds to" relationship. The claims map is roughly chronological from top to bottom, allowing a person to view the progression of ideas during the design. A division is shown between the early analytic exploration of the design space and the later synthetic integration of ideas.

Sutcliffe and Carroll [1999] defined claims maps in terms of the historical reflections. They defined claims maps as "a series of claims which share a common theoretical base and problem initiation" with relationships stemming from factoring or from empirical investigation. Claims maps allow designers to trace versions of claims through their histories, allowing a designer to probe the original purposes and motivations behind a claim. Claims maps were visually depicted by a collection of claims nodes consisting of 2–3 word features, each with a single upside and a single downside, connected by undirected links between claims (though one would expect the relationship to lead from the older claim to the newer one).

Claims maps, as defined in Wahid and McCrickard [2006], are a visual representation technique used to depict a particular state of a design, leverages our set of ten *claim relationships* to make explicit the connections between claims to emphasize the role each claim play within the overall design. Originally defined and exemplified as an engineering method, in our own experiences claims maps proved more useful as part of a design technique—elucidating goals in system design throughout the design process.

Claims maps consist of three parts, roughly corresponding to Norman's [1986] stages of design as instantiated in usability engineering [Rosson and Carroll, 2002]. The first part describes the problem, to motivate the need for system redesign. Claims emphasize consequences of features that exist in the current approach to accomplishing particular goals. The second part describes high level activities accomplished with the new interface. Activities can build upon existing activities or can be new ideas. The third part consists of information claims (that describe methods for presenting information to a user) and interaction claims (portraying ways to manipulate the system) that instantiate the activity claims. Problem claims connect to activities seen as potential solutions, which in turn, connect to information and interaction claims.

The Wahid version of a claims map consists of nodes connected by directional links (see Figure 4.4). Each node contains the title or feature of a claim. The associated upsides and downsides for each claim are not directly represented in the diagram itself, but are attached as additional information along with the claims map. This allows designers to consider the roles for the claims and to suggest new claims with only a view of the artifacts and their connections to other artifacts. If a

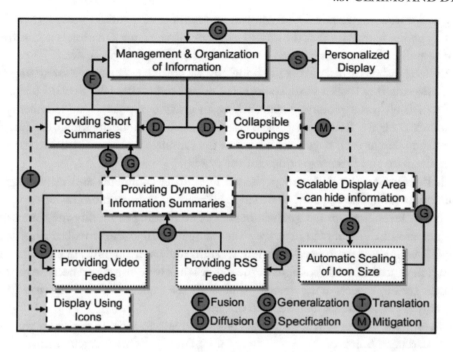

**Figure 4.4:** Claims map for the SideShow system [Cadiz et al., 2002], extracted from the paper on the system by a student design team (from Wahid, 2011).

designer wants to probe the reasoning behind a claim, the list of full claims (with upsides, downsides, etc.) is available to them.

As with many design techniques, claims maps require buy-in from the development team as to their importance—often by designating a usability engineer to maintain a claims map (as with Compendium graphs [Conklin, 2005; Culmsee and Awati, 2011]). Claims maps require a non-trivial amount of time and skill to construct and use, but by centering regular meetings around the creation and connection of claims, claims maps can emerge as natural extensions of meeting work products. The claims map promises to leverage a designer's natural tendency to think of feature consequences and synthesize these consequences into an explicit overview of a particular design state—moving from considering the minute details of a system to reflecting on the major issues. Its utility is further increased as it is updated as newer iterations of a project emerge or a designer's conceptualization of the system changes.

Maintaining the representation also allows for focused discussion to take place regarding the work. Team members can reference the claims map to talk about issues such as task coverage or the potential negative effects of a particular feature. Decisions can be made and the rationale can be reflected within the claims map. However, using such an approach requires designers actively engage in creating and modifying claims. The frequency and number of iterations must also be determined appropriately by the team such that the cost of maintaining the representation is minimized and the benefits to overall project are maximized—a potentially difficult balancing act.

To understand the utility of this methodology, we created claims maps for an ongoing development effort—the bug tracker visualization tool referenced earlier (the Social Health Overview tool). The tool itself was a prototype approaching an evaluation phase. One member of the team (Wahid) collected claims from the interface creation phase over four iterations, encouraging other members of the team at each stage to think about the rationale that contributed to the system and to consider alternate and future directions for the system.

Each iteration of the claims map yielded interesting comments and results regarding the bug visualization tool. The acquired knowledge allowed us to learn more about each aspect at a finer granularity level. Perhaps the greatest benefit of continuing to modify the claims map was a perceived increase in the ability to articulate the rationale behind the visualization. Although the problem claims remained unchanged, the design claims underwent significant changes. These were refined to better describe certain portions of the tool. Claims were also added because the team failed to account for certain aspects of the design—a possible consequence of our being too familiar with the design and bypassing details that seemed obvious.

To investigate how experienced designers would react to such an approach we interviewed five HCI researchers. Some of the interviewees were familiar with claims, but none of them had heard of claims maps prior to the interview. The semi-structured interviews involved showing the claims maps and full claims for the visualization tool and asking for comments. Discussion points included the structure, usage, and utility of the representation as well as claims and relationships. While "creativity" was not directly mentioned as a discussion point, this analysis focuses on the creative aspects that emerged in the interviews.

We initially asked the designers to take a look at the claims map and reflect on the system based on the map. The general organization of the claims map into three sections was found beneficial although some were unclear about how the Social Health Overview tool problem claims really linked to the activity claims for the visualization. The activity claims gave an overview of the general tasks afforded by the visualization and their connections to information and interaction claims formed a hierarchy that decomposed many aspects of the design.

Two researchers mentioned they found the use of claims relationships within the structure of claims maps to reveal further insight because of a sense of coverage. For instance, in reference to a claim about querying for bugs an interviewee mentioned she would "not see how querying for bugs might be instantiated". Her concern was that without seeing the relationships she could imagine querying for bugs being a textual search, when in fact that was not part of the system. She concluded the claims maps, and in particular the relationships, easily allowed her to understand each claim's role in the design—and they pointed her to a missing feature that should be included in a future tool iteration.

The structure can be valuable when it comes to explaining the current state of the design. One participant viewed the claims map as a useful conversation prop. He believed a claims map had the capability to act as an aid when describing an interface to someone else and that it could lead to more focused questions about various aspects. Questions about the way something is represented in the map may even lead to clarifications or modifications. A claims map can not be a correct or complete map, but rather a representation that could be used to integrate new members into the team, inspire reflections about the current state of the system, or start conversations about new directions for the system.

The claims and relationships record a form of rationale. The interviewees noted it did provide some useful insight which could help one familiarize themselves with a system. One participant noted, "the idea of spelling things out like this at some level can help you think about the decisions that you've made…" For example, an interviewee found great utility in using one of the relationships types because it directly connected problems associated with the system and the attempted solutions—implicitly demonstrating the rationale for why each solution was tried. Another researcher noted anyone unfamiliar with the system could look at the positive and negative effects encapsulated in a claim and make a judgment as to why a claim is used. Such a bird's eye view also has the ability to show details left out or not thought of by designers initially. Previously missed critical activities that should be supported and glaring downsides of features may be realized, showing how claims maps point to potential future steps.

We were also able to identify potential problems and drawbacks with claims maps. Some of the information in the claims map may be hard to understand. Two participants mentioned some acquired insight can be highly context dependent—the creator of the claims map may have the best understanding of it because he or she authored it. Outsiders unfamiliar with the domain or the terminology associated with a system may not be able to immediately grasp key concepts in the claims map. Some of these issues can be handled through the way the claims are authored—especially the granularity of the claims. Claims maps provide one perspective into a design and we can understand it leaves out other aspects of a system researchers may like to see. While looking at a claims map a researcher stated, "the point of it is not a visual layout, although it makes it easier to comprehend what you've got so far…but to start evaluating whether your system is emphasizing the most important things and you need outside information for that I think". Another researcher mentioned the claims map focused on providing an overview of the system, but did not provide anything about the user. Knowing how many users there are, their roles, and how they relate to one another was one of his concerns. For example, one of the things he would like to see is whether a user would engage in all the activities afforded by the system or just particular ones. When asked whether designers would be willing to use claims some of the interviewees were not quite sure. One summarized her thoughts by saying, "in an ideal world maybe". For one of her own projects, she wanted to make everything transparent and be able to show her reasoning because ultimately she wanted help from others. However, she very quickly realized she didn't have enough time to do all of that. Eventually she did only what she believed would be useful to her.

Through the interview process we were also able to gain insight into whether our argument for an iterative claims map development process would prove convincing. A researcher mentioned claims maps may be something that is done after the fact and compared it to commenting code after the code was written. Two interviewees mentioned the use of such a representation may be useful in retrospect to learn what was achieved—a situation where one is potentially looking back on an older design. However, we found it interesting that a participant mentioned the claims maps would not contain what they do if we had started creating the claims maps earlier in the visualization design project. Both of these views align with our beliefs in the benefit of using claims map within the proposed iterative methodology. Claims maps do indeed provide a view of what designers know about an interface, but the articulation of that understanding can only be developed in an iterative manner. We believe creating a single claims map early or late in a development effort provides less value than one iteratively modified throughout the project.

In summary, there were a few instances when design team members seemed inspired to think about their design in new ways. However, at times the claims map seemed to constrain thinking—limiting ideas to the nodes and paths that were present on the map or to claims information present on the claims list. The open-ended interview style was not the best approach for inspiring creativity, and the larger maps (particularly at the later iterations, when there were as many as 36 claims) may have focused discussion and narrowed the flow of ideas. Claims maps may have value as a creative design tool, but they should be paired with an appropriate creativity technique, and more thought should go into the number and type of claims and claims relationships in the map.

## 4.3.2   CLAIMS AS CREATIVE DESIGN TOOLS

The work on claims maps led us to consider ways in which visual representations of claims could help inspire creative design. This subsection examines how images that represent claims can make the claims more accessible, while not limiting—indeed, by inspiring—the creative process. A complete description of our work is described in a series of papers [McCrickard et al., 2011; Wahid et al., 2009, 2010, 2011]; an overview of our approach and findings is provided here.

With respect to user-centered HCI design, we consider this an opportunity to balance images (rich stimuli that may aid idea generation) and reusable design rationale (a cognitive tool that may aid idea assessment) in a combined artifact-based activity. We propose that, by presenting images first, the initial focus will be placed on the creation of novel ideas without immediate attention to whether ideas fit both the novel and appropriate constraints. And, presenting rationale second may allow novel ideas to be explored before being reigned in by rationale in the assessment of appropriateness.

This research avenue explores rationale and images, respectively, as complementary components for enabling the creative process. Pictures, images, and sketches have been incorporated in a number of creative design activities for their ability to stimulate divergent thinking. In creative writing, picture "sparks" are used to help inspire a new story direction [Kellaher, 1999]. The Creative Whack Pack [von Oech, 2008] and Thinkpak [Michalko, 2006] use sketches and images to encourage creative problem finding and problem reframing. Picture-based artifacts that promote creativity are also beginning to appear in HCI design methods in the form of product example pictures [Herring et al., 2009], cards that capture context [Larsson et al., 2011], and cards that capture values [Nathan et al., 2009].

Most existing image-centric creative design activities are strong on brainstorming and idea generation, but do not focus on issues of appropriateness and rationale. Our claims representation seeks to leverage and combine prior work in design rationale with creative inspiration through images by creating an image-centric artifact set. Each artifact is presented in the form of a card depicting a feature through an image and label on the front and an associated claim on the back (see Figure 4.5). We chose to place representative images and brief titles (i.e., artifact descriptions from a claim) on the front of each card, with the expectation that artifacts would be quickly recognized and designers would gain inspiration from the artifacts. In so doing, we expect that they would first consider broad possibilities of how the artifact could be used in design before being influenced by the claim on the back. However, the claim could serve as a gateway to formal design rationale, encouraging designers to consider the validity of their ideas in light of the rationale.

**Figure 4.5:** Claims cards showing pictures with labels on the front, and textual claims on the back (from McCrickard et al., 2011, and see Appendix A.19 for another example).

To explore the effectiveness of this card set, we investigated its use in a reuse-based storyboarding activity. *Storyboards* are visual narratives that include actors engaging in a series of actions toward a common goal. Typically, they consist of multiple panels made of pictures and an accompanying narrative that illustrates a temporal progression. Key aspects of a storyboard are the portrayal of time, the inclusion of people and emotions, the inclusion of text, and the level of detail [Truong et al., 2006]. Used by those involved in the creation of movies, cartoons, and commercials, they are powerful tools for thinking through and presenting the most important aspects of a narrative [Finch, 1973; Hart, 1999]. In HCI, storyboards have been used in the design process to illustrate how users may interact with a system [Buxton, 2007; Sharp et al., 2007]. Mostly used in early prototyping phases, storyboards in this domain describe the user's interaction with a system over time through a series of graphical depictions, often sketches, and units of textual narrative. Storyboards have been used to help understand the flow of the interaction scenario, to eliminate costly elements of a design, and even to decide how to pitch ideas to others [Buxton, 2007; Rosson and Carroll, 2002].

This case study investigated the use of these cards in design sessions where we asked groups of three to utilize the artifacts in creating a prototype of a notification system, tools that allow users to monitor information in dual-task situations [McCrickard et al., 2003b]. Twenty-one graduate students, randomly assigned to seven groups of three, were gathered to take part in three design sessions. Each design session featured a unique problem that called for an appropriate notification system. Example design problems included notifying nuclear plant operators of changing core temperatures, alerting passengers in airports of flight status changes, pointing commuters to empty parking lot spots, informing theme park visitors of ride wait times, and alerting students of empty spots for classes in which they wish to enroll.

All the participants were actively engaged in conducting HCI research or enrolled in a graduate HCI course at the time of the study. Their familiarity with storyboarding and claims varied. Because we target our artifacts to novice designers as well, we preferred to recruit novice designers at this stage of our investigation. Here, we report on our observations of the balance of creativity and rationale centered on the cards.

Novice designers engaged in this design activity work to familiarize themselves with the set of cards, decide on what cards might be useful for the system they wish to prototype, and construct a storyboard by placing cards together. When needed, they create their own cards to incorporate new ideas. Our observations of this activity have allowed us to understand better how these cards are able to encourage designers to balance novel ideation and grounded reasoning. We provide some examples from design sessions we ran showing how these cards impacted the construction of storyboards and provided opportunity for creative ideas along the way. The use of imagery proves to be an important segment of the activity as it is a springboard for new ideas.

One way in which they do this is by making ideas ready at hand. They enable quick digestion and recognition of reusable ideas, so much so that designers often find themselves considering all of the cards as potential candidates for their design—something often not the case when features must be read in the form of plain text. By making more features available to designers for ready consideration, we vastly expand the design space considered for assimilation in a design session. The pictures support, to a degree, universally understood communication of its direct message, the feature, and provide designers the space to incorporate the appropriate cards into their storyboard.

On the other hand, pictures also support different messages and interpretations of their contents. This proves to be another advantage of using imagery: inspiring the designers to think of other artifacts that might not have been considered, potentially leading to novel ideas. In many of our design sessions we observed participants thinking of new ideas that came from images, but were unrelated to the nature of the artifact the image was being used for. For example, in one of our design sessions we observed a group that reinterpreted a card about relating preexisting user knowledge to a notification generated by a system.

The image used for this card was a picture of a chat window showing the chat history. A participant in the group looking at the card chose to focus on the message timestamp that was contained within the chat window and proposed that the timestamp be a feature to incorporate into their storyboard. The timestamps happened to be a part of the picture, but were not necessarily there to illustrate the idea of the card. This serves to demonstrate that images can potentially inspire ideas that are beyond that of the claims themselves, leading to creative, divergent thinking patterns as well as a new source of knowledge to capture and store.

Images also afforded a platform for idea combination and domain transcendence—-both tenets of creativity. Being that the pictures—which were taken in diverse times and places—all came together on a single table top, unique comparisons and couplings became possible and even natural. Participants placed pictures side by side for comparison and on top of one another for combination. As an example of feature combination, one group discussed joining a large screen public display with a peripheral display to create a less distracting and user-driven source of information. Although the features we presented to participants were of the same domain (notification systems) we believe that there is promise in presenting an even more diverse set of images to designers to enable novel combinations.

The textual claims on the back of the cards serve as important ways for designers to consider the utility of the reusable ideas to gauge how appropriate they are. Whenever designers need more information or have doubts about how to use an artifact, claims serve as a way of describing the artifact and its utility. The claim tradeoffs play a vital role is allowing designers to decide whether the artifact should be used in a design.

Designers turn to the textual claim when debating the impact of a feature—especially high impact negative ones that they may not have realized. In one instance we observed a designer become aware of a claim downside articulating that a notification generated by the system might be missed by the user. The designer immediately found another card that might mitigate the effects of this downside. Claim tradeoffs also aid in deciding between cards when alternatives present themselves. The advantage in having the textual claim is that it can provide designers with rationale-based design concerns that they have possibly not thought of to challenge or counter their own interpretation of the card—providing an alternative perspective to the consideration of the card. Ultimately, the presence of textual claim information makes the designers more aware of the need to consider carefully the reasons for including a feature in a design.

Creating new cards to capture new ideas in the form of pictures and claims is also an important part of the activity. In the sessions we ran, 3 new cards were created. We found that cards are often created as a result of an idea that was inspired by another card, however, it would be hard to identify whether it is solely because of the image or the associated claim as well. In one instance we observed a session in which the group decided to create a new card based on a card about graphical information. Because they wanted to create a system that also incorporated geospatial location, they decided to create a new card about geospatial representation of information. A group drew a picture of a map with various points of interest within it and created a claim that was largely a more specified version of the claim used for graphical information. Their need to refer to the other card demonstrated that they wanted to maintain the same level of scope, making it generic and trying not to over-specify the card so that its potential reuse would not be restricted. Thus, the authoring of the claim was influenced by the claims that were already around them. While we see that new ideas can arise, we notice that these ideas are often grounded in other artifacts that inspired the designers. While creative thought inspired by the graphical information imagery provided a springboard for knowledge capture, the rationale ensured the designers considered the consequence of the new feature. The burdens of creating a new card in terms of content might have been lowered by introducing the a simple structure card structure, but we noticed that other factors such as the designer's own knowledge and confidence in themselves influence whether a card is created. Ultimately, the storyboard is constructed by choosing relevant cards, sequencing them according to a determined task flow, and then writing an accompanying narrative or scenario for each segment of the storyboard to solve the given design problem. We acknowledge the final product of this activity is not traditional storyboard as it does not enforce sketching. However, elements such as actors and the portrayal of time are still embodied within the narrative.

The design process undertaken by our participants revealed an interplay between image-inspired creativity and claims-based argumentation. Designers engaged in exploring new ways to combine cards together to create new functionality—although with limitations on the types of creative behaviors that were exhibited. New claims seemed to draw from the existing claims cards, as extensions, simplifications, or combinations of claims that were already present. It is important to note that designers did move beyond the individual cards to focus on the system as a whole—testing out creative new task flows that result from new combinations and sequences of claims.

The overarching belief emerging from this exploration of image-based claims is that the combination of images and claims encourages designers to brainstorm new ideas and balance prior rationale at appropriate times of an early design session. Reusing past ideas is important, but it is the application of these ideas in new ways and forms that may bring out potentially innovative solutions. Of course, great care must be taken to identify the appropriate times to use claims, and the appropriate formats (e.g., image-based, through a tool or visualization) that will drive the appropriate design behavior—whether it be creative design, scientific design, or engineering design. Chapter 5 speculates on some emerging directions for using claims in design.

# CHAPTER 5

# Looking Forward

## THE EVOLVING FACE OF CLAIMS

The changing face of human-computer interaction—as it evolves to a place better suited for a moniker like human-centric computing or human-centered informatics—creates a moving target for knowledge capture and design rational for the discipline. Claims, along with issues and patterns, have shifted in their form and usage as well, and they (and their successors) will continue to do so to match the changing needs of the discipline. The ideas in this chapter apply to knowledge capture and design rationale generally, although I focus on features found in claims that are particularly well suited to solve many of the emerging problems of HCI.

To understand how knowledge capture and design rationale may evolve in the future in HCI, it is useful to look at the related discipline of software engineering and explore its similarities and differences—particularly as software engineering as a discipline is only a decade or two older than HCI and has had similar growth pains. The preface and introduction of Rationale-based Software Engineering book [Burge et al., 2008] distinguish design rationale in software engineering from design rationale in other fields. The big difference seems to be in the certainty embedded in the rationale. Design rationale in software engineering seeks to establish a position of truth, rooted in optimal (and optimizable) functionality of the computer—comparable to the nature of physical artifacts, as seen in other fields. In contrast, design rationale in usability engineering (and even more so in the broader discipline of HCI) seeks to provide pointers toward the "right" directions—through methods, approaches, or lessons learned—that should be considered in the design process.

Patterns came to HCI from software engineering (and from architecture before that). The question about the difference between claims and patterns question has been discussed frequently in the literature [Dearden and Finlay, 2006; Sutcliffe, 2002; Wania, 2008], with the following distinctions emerging. Claims are hypothetical, intended to be debated and changed based on the context. They are smaller than patterns, and many (most!) lack the rigor that are found in established patterns libraries—but those traits also make them easier to process and change as well. Patterns purport to capture a version of "truth": knowledge that has been agreed upon by a community after a great many instantiations and studies and experiments and such. They include a statement of a problem, with specific examples of the solution captured by the pattern.

For a discipline like HCI, in which changes in context have great influence over the way a user interface should look and act, it seems that claims often would be the better choice for uncertain situations when user behavior is not fully understood. Patterns seem well-suited for HCI sub-domains like web development, in which there often can be an assumption that a typical individual working alone at a desktop or laptop machine is seeking to accomplish a task. One should also be careful of the word "typical", which often refers to a person that has close to 20/20 vision (perhaps corrected), cognitive skills sufficient to process a fairly complex screen of information, motor skills sufficient to use a mouse and keyboard, and some experience using a web browser. But as soon as those typical traits are violated in your target user population, or as soon as you start designing for noisy or busy or mobile situations, or when you're seeking to do something very different with your interface, it is necessary to question the truths—a strength of claims.

Even a repository of web design patterns like van Duyne's Design of Sites [van Duyne et al., 2002] is lauded not because it preaches HCI standard practices but because it discusses how to design (e.g., how to promote e-commerce, how to settle on a page layout, how to customize for mobile devices). It includes checklists and is rooted in context, allowing the reader to decide what's relevant. Most of the HCI patterns books focus on a particular domain of interfaces (e.g., web sites, mobile platforms), allowing the patterns authors to limit the contextual scope and create more applicable patterns.

The key elements about claims that will be reflected in the future of knowledge capture and design rationale in UE and HCI is that they are hypothetical, subject to change based on changes in context, advances in knowledge, and retargeting of product design. They are more flexible than design rationale methods from software engineering and other fields, reflecting the flexible nature of the field of HCI. But that then makes the creation of claims libraries or other reuse repositories much more difficult–one must balance correctness with hypothesis, permanence with flexibility.

Issues and IBIS seek to address an overlapping but different set of problems than HCI: those related to planning, collaboration, and complex "wicked" problems that change as a solution develops. As such, issues are highly interconnected, and are often not meaningful without the connections to other issues. IBIS approaches to design have gravitated from Rittel's original vision to one focused on building a graph of issues require an expert (or expert training) to guide the activity toward one of common understanding. Patterns are intended to have meaning individually, and claims can be standalone (but only if well crafted)—but all three can benefit from rich connections with appropriate links between them.

There are indications that these knowledge capture approaches are drawing from each other. There certainly seem to be efforts to make patterns more claims-like, such as the pre-patterns work to make use of early versions of patterns [Saponas et al., 2006]. (See an example in A.16.) Similarly, there have been efforts to formalize claims with more structure and rigor so that they are more patterns-like [Chewar, 2005; Sutcliffe, 2000]. Differences among claims, patterns, and issues stem more from the ways in which they have evolved and have been used, and not because of their inherent structure. But it seems unlikely that they will merge; rather, different communities will necessarily adopt the knowledge capture approach that they need to communicate, share knowledge, and advance their discipline.

A lot of so-called "truth" in interface design goes away when the context changes—and not just the context of work, but also the users (in terms of experience and expectations). That doesn't mean it is a bad idea to seek to capture design truths, just that they should be treated with scientific skepticism when encountered in a new design problem. Capabilities of humans can differ depending on user population characteristics, as can the situations in which an interface will be used. My current thought is to use claims in this way: making it clear in design activities that they are meant to be challenged and questioned, not taken at face value—the first future work example in Chapter 4 gives an example of this approach. It's there that I think the greatest value for claims (and the distinguishing value from other knowledge capture approaches) can be realized.

While each of the visions in this chapter is framed in terms of claims, the "correct" way to structure the knowledge will evolve as the visions are realized—and will evolve as the discipline of HCI continues to evolve. I considered categorizing these visions in terms of engineering, science, or creative design approaches that were described in earlier chapters (certainly some seem better suited for these categories than others). But most of them cross over categories, and it is here that I see the greatest value: it will help the discipline of HCI to coalesce if there are approaches to design that can bring people with different skill sets together to solve important problems.

## 5.1    MULTIDISCIPLINARY RESEARCH WITH CLAIMS

The nature of claims—brief statements that balance the upsides and downsides of a focal point— provide the opportunity to use them to encourage knowledge transfer across disciplines. While many of the early books and papers on claims in HCI focused on a single discipline, there is opportunity for broader focus. Much as Toulmin's original vision for a claim as part of argumentation shifted from a narrow discipline-focused view in *The Uses of Argument* to a broader multidisciplinary view in his later works like *Cosmopolis*, claims as applied to design and HCI has the opportunity to expand in its focus as the discipline of HCI continues to evolve to encompass multiple disciplines.

The focus on multiple disciplines is not intended to exclude the use of claims within a discipline. Indeed, a well-defined discipline provides an opportunity for a claims library rooted in deeply researched claims—similar to the patterns libraries for fields like architecture and software engineering. A claims library can provide short cues or reminders about critical issues within a field, serving as a starting point for research and design.

However, claims in multidisciplinary projects can be used to capture and share knowledge across the disciplines. Exercising the hypothetical nature of claims, it is valuable to look at situations in which there are differences in opinions about ways to proceed in the design task. The nature of a claim could guide participants in a design session to suggest ideas, debate upsides and downsides, and probe avenues for exploration external to the design session (e.g., experiments to undertake, documentation to read). Connections established between the claims could reflect ways to mitigate downsides of the claims, to show sequences of steps, or to show alternative ways to accomplish a goal.

As an example from a project currently under way, a multidisciplinary team is creating a mobile job monitoring interface for young people with moderate to severe cognitive disabilities. The young people often cannot remember at a later time what parts of a job environment they did and did not like, so the job placement assistants need a way to collect data at frequent intervals that does not require an assistant to be present at all times. Each contributing discipline has its own needs and concerns: the programmers have knowledge about available hardware and its strengths and limitations, the assistants to the people with disabilities know the capabilities of the people from human intervention (but not technology intervention), our usability engineers understand performance capabilities for a "typical" person but have limited knowledge about people with cognitive disabilities. These multidisciplinary projects tend to be heavy in domain knowledge, drawing together multiple domains with their own needs. Many of the mobile interface claims just don't hold when designing for people with cognitive disabilities: button sizes have to be bigger (sometimes with only a single "button"), the number of simultaneous choices have to be limited to two or at most three, and single-switch scanning should redundantly be employed to communicate on-screen text. In addition, the experiences have to be tailored differently: repetition in experience and questioning is often more important than reflection, and great care must be taken in the use of appropriate symbol sets.

This type of project is multidisciplinary in that it is not rooted in any one discipline—it is not the case that a discipline is "borrowing" knowledge from another, but rather there are unique problems that can only be addressed adequately if knowledge from all of the disciplines is integrated. An expert at mobile interface design would almost have to "start over", throwing away (or, at a minimum, reconsidering) all knowledge about how to design the interface. A caregiver needs to rethink the way questions are asked if humans are replaced by technology. By using claims to connect the disciplines, the design team can capture their concerns succinctly and move toward a solution with broader knowledge and confidence.

## 5.2 NEUTRAL CLAIMS

Even though claims seek to hypothesize rather than expound the truth, there's always a danger that they will be read as truth. A key step: Defining claims to getting rid of upsides and downsides—they are too polarizing and can lead to bias. Replace them with bullets or (partial) ratings to allow the designer to decide what's an upside and downside within the context of the design or to rate them based on the current project's needs. (One person's bug is another person's feature.) Thus, leave open for debate whether an effect is an upside or downside. For example, a simple claim for cognitive disabilities is:

> **Highlighting words on a screen and presenting them with a synthesized voice:**
>
> + Provides multiple channels to gain understanding of the on-screen information
>
> − BUT is not suitable for rapid recognition of and reaction to urgent information.

However, at times the upside might be undesirable, or the downside might be desirable. One modification for a claims, bringing it closer to its original intent as a falsifiable hypothesis that can be used as the basis for collaborative discussions about wicked problems. To do so, we suggest changing the structure somewhat, extending the *interface artifact* focus to include interface use context, other artifacts, actors and their characteristics, and other elements of interest in interface development. We will augment each claim with supporting material, such as links to papers, interviews, experiments, or quotes that support the hypothesized claim. And we will seek to remove the somewhat biasing upsides and downsides, since these are situationally dependent. (A downside in one situation might be an upside in another—in the provided claim, perhaps fixing the communication speed may be ideal for some users but frustrating for others.) An example claim in this new form would look as follows:

**Highlighting words on a screen and presenting them with a synthesized voice:**

- Provides redundant understanding cues
- Fixes communication speed with reading speed

Again, this is a fairly simple claim—most will have many more bulleted features, references, pictures, etc. By crafting the claim differently, it encourages discussion and debate as to its merits. There are external references to outside documents that can be used to assess quality of the claim and need for further study—e.g., a weak (or no) reference suggests an implementation or study might be needed. However, the limited communities of users of these approaches highlights the necessity to show (and sometimes hide!) knowledge appropriately during the design process.

## 5.3    IDENTIFYING RELATIONSHIPS BETWEEN CLAIMS

The ability to understand the alternative, complementary, and contrasting ideas is key to enabling design. It's particularly hard to do that at the level of a paper or a product—their nuances make it hard to compare them in a meaningful way. It's not easy to do so with claims, but at least it seems possible. Visionaries like Otlet and Nelson recommend letting people identify relationships between claims-like chunks of knowledge. At the heart of Wahid's thesis was the notion of claims relationships. Mathematical models can refine and quantify the relationships to highlight them to designers (e.g., Chewar's approach to index based on critical parameters then use experimental results or designer surveys to rate the claims). There seems to be progress toward this goal.

A claims library stores claims and maintains claim relationships between claims. This imposed structure creates a network of claims designers can navigate through using relationships to find what is needed [Wahid et al., 2004]. Additionally, it encourages designers to imagine how disparate ideas can be combined together to form a coherent design. Such prior work on the development of claims and the claims library has shown great promise, yet lacking are large claims repositories with sufficient associated tools and processes to guide and inspire future design. Claims libraries have been speculated and created previously (e.g., Payne et al., 2003; Rosson and Carroll, 2002; Sutcliffe, 2002), but never before with the highly accessible claims, and never before with the high degree of interconnectivity as described in this subsection. Relationships are obviously core to IBIS descriptions of design, and relationships have been noted as important for patterns as well [Tidwell, 2005].

Systems can be designed and analyzed using a representative set of new and reused claims [Rosson and Carroll, 2002]. Within this collection, claims form specific types of interactions with one another. Claim relationships make these interactions explicit to designers. Our previous research has identified an initial set of relationships to help categorize these interactions based on design associations [Wahid et al., 2004]—although we anticipate adding categories based on user skills and limitation type, workplace context, technology platform, and more. Example relationships include:

- *Postulation/Prediction:* the relationships that exist between claims depicting problems in the current situation and claims depicting potential solutions for the new design.

- *Generalization/Specification:* claims can be written in different scopes—general claims encompass larger concepts while specific claims have a narrower scope.

- *Mitigation:* each specific downside of a claim can be mitigated by another claim.

Our research team defines a *claims map* as a conceptual form of design representation leveraging both the simplicity of claims and the descriptive capability of selected claim relationships [Wahid and McCrickard, 2006]. Claims maps provide a method for representing a design using the collection of claims by describing how each claim fits into the larger system being created. Its structure encompasses claims from requirements analysis, activity design, and information and interaction design—giving the chance for one to quickly understand the rationale for using certain claims in each design phase. Within educational settings we have found claims maps to more explicitly articulate claim types, system goals, and future areas of the system to target for evaluation and redesign. To provide full support to designers wishing to take advantage of this representation, we propose a visualization tool, highly integrated with the claims library, to allow a user to write their own claims and reuse claims from the library in maintaining a claims map. There are three potential benefits to creating and using this tool:

1. Support for the articulation of an interface through tradeoffs, rationale, goals, and features during development—a manifestation of a fundamental design task.

2. Increased reuse during the development phase, eliminating the perception of reuse being a noble, but burdening task. A claims map tool must allow users to engage their own knowledge as they work, but "run into" reusable knowledge from the claims library when most appropriate.

3. Create a constant source of fresh content for the library by storing the newly created claims in the claims map for others to reuse.

Claims maps show potential in becoming design representations that can be created easily in an iterative manner. To ensure we understand the long-term benefits of utilizing such documentation we must continue to develop these ideas and explore their use within workshop and course settings.

## 5.4    CLAIMS-BASED DESIGN APPROACHES

To this point we have described the knowledge structures that we expect will assist in collaborative design and development of interfaces for people with cognitive disabilities, toward a growing collection of claims that provide a strong basis for knowledge capture, maintenance, and reuse. However, to further our knowledge-centric collaboration initiative a key concern is the absence of aspects that allow for the use of guiding design processes—particularly those that support collaborative theories—toward supporting the integration of many design ideas in a focused design effort. We feel a need to consider how core theories of design will integrate with our knowledge capture approach, allowing academics to analyze the approaches, identify paths for interface creation, and create their own interfaces to support people with cognitive disabilities.

To that end, we suggest a concept of *knowledge-centric collaboration*: a theory-based staged design approach in which activities of designers must focus on development of knowledge that can be *captured*, *substantiated*, *compared*, and *communicated*. As detailed in this subsection, these stages (and relationships between them) mirror fundamental aspects of existing theories (e.g., Clark, 1996; Halverson, 1994; Harrison et al., 1995). An example of knowledge-centric collaboration is scenario-based design (SBD), which centers the activity of interface design around scenarios and claims [Rosson and Carroll, 2002]. But we would be remiss if we did not point out that knowledge capture structures like claims are well suited for other knowledge-centric collaboration approaches as well. We endeavor to do that by exploring how to define and reify this type of collaboration.

A first goal is *to establish a theory of knowledge-centric collaboration* based on the design capture and reuse framework that claims enable. We intend to borrow concepts from particular design theories and instantiate them within the tool in the form of a newer representation coupled by methodological steps. While the theories we choose to investigate may change or grow based on Phase 1 activities, two well-established theories in HCI that seem of particular relevance to claims are *common ground* [Clark, 1992, 1996] and *distributed cognition (DCog)* [Hutchins, 1995]. This subsection will examine how those theories may be of use in problem design and analysis—particularly when dealing with a diverse set designers who might not be co-located and who might be working asynchronously.

Common ground, as introduced by Herbert Clark [Clark, 1992, 1996], is a theory that describes successful communication between people. Common ground can be characterized by the following definition: "a proposition $p$ is established as common ground if all the individuals communicating know $p$ and they all know that they know $p$". As people communicate with each other, mechanisms that place people on the same page become critical. Key aspects of common ground

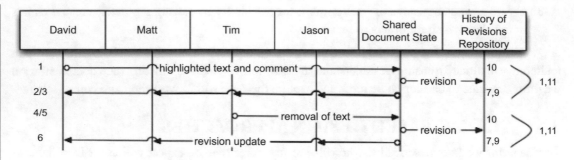

**Figure 5.1:** A possible design representation for distributed cognition (DCog) that leverages claims. Propagation of information is shown using the arrows that transition between people and the system. Relevant claims are attached using index numbers at the right side.

map directly to our identified stages of knowledge-centric collaboration: common ground's visibility is much like our capture stage—both considering how researchers work together toward establishing a common, shared knowledge unit; common ground's sequentiality and reviewability map to our comparison stage—in which researchers will iterate on existing knowledge structures toward a deeper understanding of their nature and relationships. While beneficial, the common ground theory has been posited to be incomplete for certain types of analyses, requiring further extension and customization, and in need of support for asynchronous communication [Birnholtz et al., 2005; Carroll et al., 1992]. Our claims-based collaboration approach, focused on shared knowledge, has promise to lessen these effects.

Although today's notion of distributed cognition is relatively recent [Hutchins, 1995], the theory arose from the need to analyze how information processing and problem solving occurred across units of analysis, incorporating both tools and other people that may be involved. The information might be held by an artifact that belongs to a system or might be passed on to another individual. Thus, DCog treats actors as well as artifacts as cognitive beings. While it might seem DCog can only be used to analyze an existing system, it can also yield benefit to other stages of design during the development process [Halverson, 1994]. However, DCog has been criticized for its flexibility in the work products that result from any analysis [Carroll et al., 1992].

Our initial meta-analysis of the use of such collaborative design theories leads us to believe that there are elements of each that can be borrowed and instantiated within the design approaches that should be supported. This will directly lead to a modified design representation beyond claims maps that continues to leverage claims, but also supports the use of such design theories. For example, Figure 5.1 demonstrates a possible representation developed for a DCog analysis. Key aspects of the diagram are the explicit representation of actors and the information propagation among the actors. Figure 5.2 illustrates a variation of a claims map that supports a common grounded analysis. In this example, the claims are tagged with the grounding constraints that they support in the system. Additionally, information about the participants is provided through a 0–1 scale. These

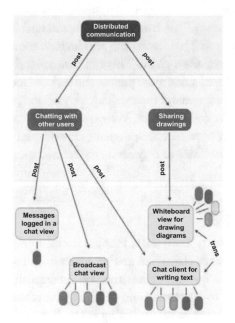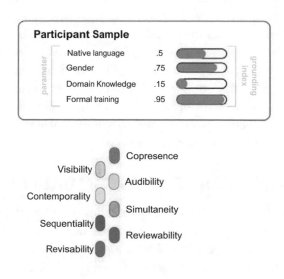

**Figure 5.2:** A representation developed to represent the grounding constraints for Common Ground. The claims are tagged with constraints that are accounted for in the system. Additionally, information about participants is provided using a 0–1 scale.

characteristics can be considered as potential artifacts of a new representation building on top of claims maps for practitioners to focus collaboration around.

To fully define a new representation and, consequently collaborative tool, we must continue to analyze other theories of collaboration. By performing a meta-analysis, such as the one described using DCog and common ground, we can fully characterize the features, steps, and artifacts needed for a new design representation. These new representations allow for knowledge-centric collaboration to occur under the umbrella of claims using various methodological perspectives drawn from research. Such an effort can put the theories into practice and provide better definitions for the use of the methodologies—potentially alleviating some of the limitations identified with the theories.

The second goal of this effort is *to facilitate collaboration among multiple designers* in an effort to further our knowledge-centric collaboration initiative. Currently, our model supports an asynchronous method of design—claims are created, stored, and later accessed by others for further design work. This new approach must enable practitioners to work together to further benefit the projects being developed—building on the four-stage knowledge-centric collaboration approach introduced earlier in this subsection. Support for multi-person and synchronous interaction will allow for groups of designers to communicate, make decisions, and modify the design representation on the fly, enabling a focus on four key activities important in both design and collaboration—capture, substantiation, comparison, and communication. While communication can occur verbally because designers will be collocated, further support for recording some of the communication will enable practitioners to continue their work over a longer period of time. This record can also include some of the reasoning for why a decision was made to include or exclude a claim. This can consequently also improve the quality of the claims being developed and stored since more people will be involved in their creation and usage. These advancements will focus designers on the methodology of design rather than trying to thinks of ways to overcome hurdles in collaboration. We expect that these approaches, or ones similar to them, will enable a diverse set of researchers, domain experts, practitioners, supporters, and friends of people with cognitive disabilities to contribute to technological solutions to improve their quality of life.

## 5.5  IDENTIFYING QUALITY CLAIMS

Creating claims is fairly easy. But creating quality claims—particularly ones that are useful to the designer and to others down the road—is very challenging. Since claims are used in brainstorming, there necessarily will be a great many claims of questionable quality: claims that are incomplete, ill-conceived, too specific to a single problem or domain, or too general to be of use. Quite often, claims are viewed to be ephemeral, throw-away knowledge chunks with no lasting value. But there are approaches with which a determined company or community can create a library of quality claims that can be used and reused in design situations.

One solution for companies or groups seeking to create and maintain a quality claims library is to designate a person or group to maintain the library. This entity would work with knowledge creators—those who research ideas, create software, run usability tests, etc.—to identify claims of reasonable quality. This entity might encourage others in the organization to author quality claims, or it may simply author the claims themselves. Just as many users of Compendium recommend expert assistance in the creation of IBIS graphs (see Chapter 3), the identification of one or more claims experts has the potential to lead to a high-quality claims library.

Another solution is to embed into a corporate culture the need to generate claims as part of everyone's job. Claims within such an organization would truly become the lingua franca, the shared language that becomes part of meetings, writeups, and other communications. There would have to be steps to train everyone to know and understand how to create and use claims, but the resulting claims library could make available lots of possibilities for the organization.

A third solution is to let the masses decide on the best claims through crowdsourcing or votes or other recommendations. Ideally, the high-quality claims would receive the better recommendations and would then become more accessible. By rewarding the people who author high-quality claims, and by rewarding the people who vote for or comment on claims, there would be incentive for people to create quality claims and to advertise their use.

The choice of method from among these (or others) depends on the target audience for the claims library. For example, Wikipedia has a large and dedicated following by people who appreciate its size and breadth, but many people choose to use a more professionally-vetted source for which they can be assured a certain level of quality, consistency, and correctness. Techniques for creating and maintaining a claims library would vary whether created within a closed community like a company or an open community like an open software group. Whichever method is undertaken, there need to be reward structures to ensure that the claims library is appropriately populated and maintained.

## 5.6   AUTOMATIC EXTRACTION OF CLAIMS FROM DATABASES

One of the big problems with claims—and all knowledge capture and design rationale—is in the challenge of knowledge identification from repositories of data. Automatic extraction of claims from these databases has promise to address this problem. I use the term "databases" broadly, to include professional papers, chat/meeting logs, blogs, case studies, scenario libraries, or other such repositories. If done with high quality, it would cut down on the high costs (and low immediate benefits) of generating claims sets.

Numerous people have pursued or seem to be pursuing this idea. Janet Burge is working on this to extract software engineering rationale from bug reports for computer programs [Burge, 2012]. Evolving knowledge about when bugs happen and how they are addressed reflect the changing nature of a software system. Ray McCall is examining extraction of categorized knowledge from response logs for community events [McCall, 2012]. For example, community reactions to planned logging of a forest in a green area can be aggregated to understand demographic breakdowns of support and opposition to the plans.

These evolving approaches show promise for certain categories of claims (and design rationale). Yet there is a danger in assuming that the approaches will identify the "best" claims, or the "right" claims, for the situation. There seems to be great benefit in the *process* of claims identification—going through the steps to understand the nature of the repository beyond the claims that are extracted from it. Ideally, a tool should assist a person in browsing and learning about the database, rather than seeking to provide the answers. The approaches described here seem best suited to providing starting points for knowledge capture rather than serving as a complete solution.

## 5.7   CLAIMS FOR EVERYONE

The previous subsections in this chapter—and indeed most of the previous chapters in this book— outlined ways in which academics, researchers, and practitioners would benefit from a knowledge repository of knowledge about cognitive disabilities. But many of the approaches detailed previously are not highly accessible to most people (at least not without a trained HCI professional with knowledge about the area). To ensure broad dissemination of the findings, we suggest online repositories of materials that are widely accessible—topically focused to provide pathways to important knowledge for all stakeholders.

For example, when considering a knowledge repository that would support people with cognitive disabilities, it should provide support for the programmer seeking to build an interface for a friend, for the family member wondering whether to invest in a new technology, for a person with a cognitive disability looking to make sense of available technology options. Such a repository would provide access to the claims, but also to the literature behind them, e.g., the people making the claims, the papers that discuss them, interviews or design logs that highlight the motivation.

One way to accomplish this goal is through *card sets*, decks of cards with both visual and textual representations of the cognitive disability claims. The form factor is similar to the Otlet vision of knowledge on a 3 × 5 in notecard—easily digestible by a reader, even when there are lots of cards to browse. Modern efforts include IDEO's method cards [IDEO, 2003], von Oech's whack pack [2008], and Larsson et al.'s context cards [2011]—and our own PIC-UP card set, based on previous efforts from our lab that resulted in knowledge cards to assist designers of notification systems that was featured in papers and conference workshops [McCrickard et al., 2010; Wahid et al., 2010, 2011]. See A.19 for an example from PIC-UP.

There should also be access to the larger, more complex claims, driven by Wikimedia or some similar Web-based wiki approach. A claims set should be seeded with some of the more substantial claims—ones that include references and links to external information showing considerable thought and reflection. Wiki-based claims should represent the most important issues for the field of cognitive disabilities. As such, the resource could not be a fully open wiki in that we will seek to maintain control over the number and quality of entries.

Perhaps most accessible would be something like a set of web pages or wiki entries for the end users and their supporters, detailing key findings in a language and style with wide availability. Readers could seek to address questions like "Do I need to buy an iPad for my autistic child"? and "What can I do to help Grandma communicate after her stroke"? not by answering the questions but by outlining the important things for the questioner to consider—whether the person with the cognitive disability falls within a reasonable skill range for a technological solution, whether the person is appropriately motivated at the current life point, whether the financial and skill outlay for the technology is reasonable and might pay off. This type of resource would enable a claims-driven skill set for addressing the problems to caregivers who are truly facing wicked problems.

At the heart of the claim is a focus on an artifact, encapsulated together with its upsides and downsides. This combination allows a person to view knowledge not as static and certain, but as a changing and hypothetical source of inspiration that is meant to be questioned, explored, and studied. Visionaries like Paul Otlet and Vannevar Bush understood the vital link that technology could play in harnessing the exploding collection of world knowledge, and modern philosophers like Toulmin create an informal path through the knowledge that allows us to construct arguments in an uncertain world. Whether we approach knowledge from a perspective of engineering, science, and creative design, or whether we approach it as a curious observer, our tools and techniques should support a questioning nature. Claims has the potential to fill that role.

# 5.8    CLAIMS INFLUENCING THE HCI DISCIPLINE

This book has sought to illustrate how claims can help in the design process for HCI from a variety of disciplinary perspectives. But regardless of whether claims evolve to be a key part of HCI design, there are lessons to take away from their definitive components that are important in any HCI effort.

A claim presents a core finding for HCI in a designer digestible format—encouraging the quick creation, assimilation, modification, and rebuttal of claims. There are situations when this format is particularly important: in collaborative design settings when rapid reaction is important, in browsing large numbers of claims, in seeking inspiration for a problem. Much as the 140 character limit in Twitter encourages a brevity of thought that has mass appeal, it is important for knowledge creators to consider how to package their findings in an accessible manner. HCI should not be reduced exclusively to a collection of tweets, but identifying an appropriate chunk of knowledge— whether it resembles an Otlet notecard, a Rittel issue, a Google search result, or a pattern or claim in one of their many formats—can provide an easy access point to HCI knowledge for designers and practitioners.

Claims include both upsides and downsides with the artifact under consideration, seeking to encourage designers to consider both its positive and negative effects. This troika of information serves to support considered thought regarding the adoption of the artifact for a design, thus avoiding situations where designers are blinded by the positive aspect of the artifact or feature. All too often in HCI, reports focus too much on the positive aspects of a design, feature, or approach (or they present neither upsides nor downsides). Leveraging the claims model in the presentation of knowledge provides readers with the balanced perspective necessary for informed decision making.

Claims embraced a hypothetical nature from its earliest instantiations. While reference to it as a *hypothesis* can suggest that the knowledge contained in the claim is not grounded or serious, the term serves to encourage those who engage with claims to consider as much why they might *not* be true as why they are true. HCI seems to be at a point at which too often researchers and practitioners take for granted the things they read rather than questioning it from a position of intellectual curiosity. Whether a claim, a report from a cognitive walkthrough, results from an experiment, or something else, it is important that we consider the knowledge that is presented as a step in a complex and ever changing problem space. The way that those in the HCI field choose to use that knowledge will encourage its growth and reuse.

# APPENDIX A

# Timeline of Advances in Claims, Patterns, and Issues

This appendix captures a temporal ordering of key advances for claims, patterns, and issues, balancing the discourse given in Chapters 2, 3, and 4. The advances feature examples adopted from the papers, books, and web sites where they originally appeared, augmented with personal experiences and other material. In the spirit of this book, the advances are in the form of *claims*, highlighting a key feature of the work, interesting and hypothetical upsides and downsides, a brief narrative, and a key example. This list is not meant to be exhaustive, containing only a fraction of the examples in this book. Rather it seeks to highlight interesting and different departures in the development and use of knowledge capture. Nor are the claims meant to be complete—they should be viewed as a starting point to discussion, toward expansion of the claim, creation of new claims, and possibly refutation of the claim or its upsides and downsides.

## A.1    TOULMIN'S CLAIMS (1958)

**claims as a tool for rhetoric and argumentation**

+ provide an informal and practical model for crafting arguments

− may provide inadequate rigor for sound arguments

Toulmin [1958] introduced the concept of uncertain, hypothetical claims into rhetoric and argumentation. Toulmin's claims are supported by data, which are connected by warrants. (Example adapted from Toulmin, 1958, p. 92.)

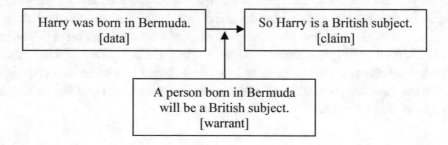

# A.2   RITTEL'S ISSUES IN IBIS (1970)

**issues as organizational atoms of IBIS-type systems**

+ provides a broadly applicable approach to wicked problems

− lacks examples that demonstrate the utility of issues

− only provides a manual approach to design (no computerization)

Kunz and Rittel [1970] articulated the key components of an issue and an issue-based information system (IBIS) in this 1970 paper, which sets for the argumentative process, the logic of issues, the structure of IBIS-type systems, and the operation of an IBIS system in a series of eleven steps. While they did not provide examples (claimed to be "forthcoming" in the paper), the figure below provides some of the core components they described.

- Issues are organizational atoms of IBIS-type systems, presented in the form of controversial questions and specific to certain situations.
- Issues are raised, argued, settled, "dodged" or substituted.
- Relationships between issues include direct successor, generalization, compatible, or incompatible (among others).
- Issues can be factual, deontic, explanatory, or instrumental.
- Other elements of IBIS-type systems include topics, questions of fact, and model problems.

## A.3  ALEXANDER ARCHITECTURAL PATTERNS (1977)

**patterns as an approach to architectural design**

+ provide a narrative, features, and illustrations to address known problems

+ link to known patterns to support assessment of alternatives

− can lack adequate evidence of the correctness of their ideas

− do not encourage formulation of new ideas or modification of existing ideas

Alexander and his colleagues presented a collection of linked *patterns* for architecture, a concept later adopted for software engineering and HCI. Most patterns included a narrative to support the need for the architectural feature, followed by a series of rules, a pictoral illustration, and a list of related patterns. The representative pictoral example below, found in Alexander et al. [1977, p. 98], is accompanied by a one-page narrative about the problems and opportunities associated with a high-speed road (including requirements that link to other transportation and population claims), a list of three rules (e.g., place high-speed roads so that at least one lies tangent to each local transport area), and references to other numbered patterns (e.g, always place roads on boundaries between sub-cultures—SUBCULTURE BOUNDARY (15)).

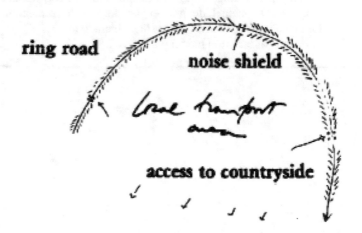

# A.4    CONKLIN ISSUES TOOL GIBIS (1988)

**a graphical tool for constructing IBIS models**

+ provides computer support for creation, searching, and compressing of IBIS models

+ adds hypertext linking to easily transition between nodes

− does not support for achieving consensus or documenting design decisions

− cannot link to external code, modules, etc.

Conklin and his colleages developed the first widely used issue-based tools, graphical IBIS (gIBIS), to provide computer support for the creation of IBIS graphs. The following image appeared in Begeman and Conklin [1988], illustrating how large portions of an issue-based map can be aggregated into a single node.

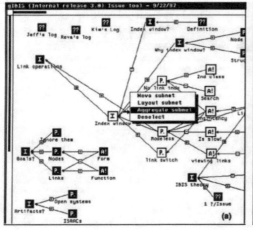
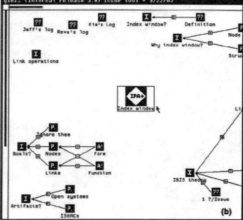

## A.5   CARROLL AND KELLOGG PSYCHOLOGICAL CLAIMS (1989)

**psychological claims in HCI**

+ articulate the claims that are embodied by artifacts

+ bridge theories in HCI with findings from psychology

− lack associated methodologies for their creation and use

Carroll and his colleagues introduced the notion of claims to HCI [Carroll and Kellogg, 1989], referring to them as *psychological claims* and presenting them as a bridge between theories about HCI and findings from psychologists about human reactions to artifacts. The example below (appearing as Table 2 in Carroll and Kellogg, 1989) shows four claims for an information authoring and retrieval system in which data are captured in stacks of virtual cards.

**Table A.1:**  Psychological Claims of Some Hypercard Techniques

|  | Goals | Planning/Acting | Evaluation |
|---|---|---|---|
| User Levels | labeled staging of system function facilitates goal identification<br><br>working on staged tasks facilitates goal mapping | staging kernel scenarios integrates basic skill<br><br>staged function and label covariation helps link plan to goals | reduced device space constrains hypothesis generation<br><br>staged function supports incremental learning |
| Examples, Built-ins | a range of concrete task instances establish a task orientation<br><br>concrete, meaningful objects suggest goals<br><br>examples facilitate goal mappings | using built-in parts simplifies plans<br><br>modifying is easier than creating from scratch | manipulating meaningful, familiar objects suggests hypotheses<br><br>learning by doing is superior to being told |
| Card Catalog Metaphor | database-as-stack simplifies goal mapping | prior | knowledge framework facilitates explanations |
| Menu Dimming |  | preempting syntactic errors reduces the amount of syntactic knowledge to be learned<br><br>backgrounding syntactic details reduces level of awareness of syntax<br><br>preempting syntactic errors avoids frustration | visual distinction between active and inactive menu items implicitly poses evaluative questions<br><br>exposure to full menus supports incidental learning |

## A.6    MCCALL TOOL SUPPORT AND ISSUES REIFICATION IN PHI (1991)

**the PHI approach to design**

+ supports a broad set of ways to raise, relate, and resolve issues

+ is supported in hypertext tools for computer-aided design and decision-making

− lacks a broad user base

− does not support distributed, synchronous collaboration and sharing of results

McCall sharpened the Rittel view of issues and IBIS in his Procedural Hierarchy of Issues (PHI) approach, as detailed in Chapter 2 and in McCall [1991]. He and his colleagues created a series of tools that leveraged the IBIS/PHI approach, enabling users to search, browse, annotate, expand, and modify an architecture knowledge base. The screenshot, courtesy of Ray McCall, shows the PHIDIAS used in the design of a moon-based habitat. Key aspects of PHIDIAS include the use of Domain-Oriented Issue Bases to show rationale for recurring issues in given application domains, and integration of supporting multimedia information with the traditional IBIS textual rationale.

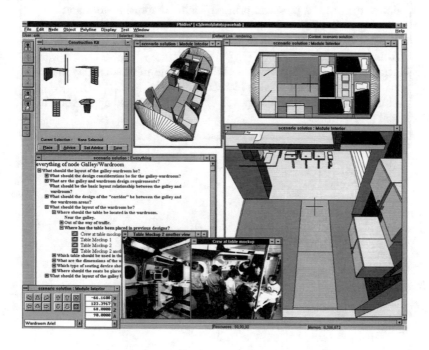

## A.7   CARROLL AND ROSSON CLAIMS IN A TASK-ARTIFACT FRAMEWORK (1992)

**claim creation as part of a task-artifact framework**

+ exposes and codifies psychological explanations for situations in scenarios

+ encourages explicit thought about situation upsides and downsides

− but may not yield claims suitable for reuse

− but no tools exist to capture this framework

Carroll and Rosson [1992] put forth a scenario-claim approach to design in which claims served to capture issues related to the contributions of artifacts in a scenario. Each claim provides a hypothesis related to some psychological consequence of a system feature, to emerge and evolve through a *claims analysis* that reflects how a claim effects users, what the positive and negatives are, and where there is potential for error. This process results in a *task-artifact framework* that shows how a knowledge base can evolve during design. An example claim, emerging from a set of scenarios about a type-and-print learning system, is given here (from Carroll and Rosson, 1992, p. 203).

decompositing "typing and printing" into component steps and training each of these in turn

+ allows a complex target objective to be systematically built up from parts

- but learners may not tolerate such rote programmes, or may make errors which corrupt what is learned

- but this organization may not facilitate retrieval and application in real task settings

# A.8    GANG OF FOUR PATTERNS (1995)

**patterns for reuse in software engineering**

+ provide proven solutions for repeatedly-encoutered problems

+ encourage reuse of successful design

− only captures a small fraction of expert knowledge

− lacks domain-specific patterns for HCI, databases, etc.

This seminal work in software engineering put forth a book of patterns—based on the principle that expert designers do not solve every problem from the beginning, but rather they repeatedly resue recurring solutions [Gamma et al., 1995]. The patterns capture four core essential elements: a name, the problem (intent and motivation), a solution (including applicability, structure, participants, collaborations, implementation, and sample code), and consequences of applying the pattern. Most patterns are around 10 pages in length; a brief synopsis of a pattern is provided here (taking only the first few lines of each category, and omitting the structure diagram and sample code).

---

BUILDER (Object Creational)

Intent: Separate the construction of a complex object from its representation so that the same construction process can create different representations

Motivation: A reader for the RTF (Rich Text Format) document exchange format should be able to convert RTF to many text formats. …

Applicability: Use the Builder pattern when the algorithm for creating a complex object should be independent of the parts that make up the object and how they're assembled …

Participants: Builder (TextConverter) specifies an abstract interface for creating parts of a Product object …

Collaborations: The client creates the Director object and configures it with the desired Builder object …

Consequences: 1. *It lets you vary a product's internal representation.* The Builder object provides the director with an abstract interface for constructing the product. …

Implementation: Typically there's an abstract Builder class that defines an operation for each component that a director may ask it to create. …

Known Uses: The RTF converter application is from ET++ …

Related Patterns: Abstract Factory (87) is similar to Builder in that it too may construct complex objects. The primary difference …

## A.9   ERICKSON AND THOMAS ACTIVITY AND DESIGN PATTERNS (1998)

> **patterns and pattern languages in HCI**
>
> + capture hypothetical activities that can introduce possible directions for development and testing
> + capture established designs that can be applied to similar situations
> − few quality HCI-related patterns have been created or used

Thirteen participants took part in a 1997 workshop held in conjunction with the ACM SIGCHI Conference. Erickson and Thomas were listed as collaboration contacts, and all authors were listed alphabetically on a SIGCHI Bulletin paper [Bayle et al., 2008]. This write-up provides the first extensive framework for studying patterns in HCI. The workshop distinguished between *activity patterns* that non-judgementally describe how things currently exist and *design patterns* that connect repeatedly encountered problems with proven solutions. Proposed uses for HCI patterns included capture and description, generalization, rhetoric, and prescriptive and predictive solutions. It was suggested that HCI patterns should have four components—problem context, forces, solution, and comments. This example pattern (one of a number of unproven activity patterns generated at the workshop) was described in Bayle et al. [2008]:

> **Clarification Graffiti**
>
> Problem context: Designers try to anticipate interaction patterns and add cues ahead of time to facilitate interaction. However, since the perspective of the user in use is different from that of the designer, the cues are never sufficient.
>
> Forces: Signage (and other cues) should be consistent to signal their relevance to the user, and to be aesthetically pleasing. Of course, this requires that signs are built ahead of time, outside of the context of use, and thus guarantees insufficiency.
>
> Solution: Allow users to add annotations to pre-designed cues.
>
> Comments: This pattern was based on the observation of a preprinted sign, near the elevator, that said 'Message Board on Ballroom Level.' Below it, someone had taped a handwritten note that said '(Go up one floor)'. …

# A.10 SUTCLIFFE AND CARROLL CLAIMS FOR ENGINEERING (1999)

**claims with added elements to capture additional situational data**

+ enable claim indexing and comparison

+ result in more uniform claim quality

− increase the complexity of the claim

This culmination of a collaboration between Sutcliffe and Carroll reframed claims into a reusable form—adding elements that make it possible to index and compare claims, to view related claims, to understand the theories that motivate the claims, and to delve deeper into claims to better understanding them. The example claim, appearing in Sutcliffe and Carroll [1999], was extracted from an evaluation of the PROUST intelligent tutoring system [Johnson, 1985]. The model served as the basis for a slightly expanded version appearing in Sutcliffe [2002].

| | |
|---|---|
| Claim ID: | plan-based error messages claim. |
| Author: | Singley, M. K.; Carroll, J. M. |
| Artifact: | PROUST Intelligent Tutoring System [Johnson, 1985] |
| Description: | system-generated error messages couched in terms of goals and plans. |
| Upsides: | brings appropriate planning abstractions to bear when they are needed. spares the learner the burden of generating explicit goal and plan descriptions |
| Downsides: | learners may develop superficial understanding when errors are not under learner control |
| Scenario: | the user is learning Pascal by going through exercises. The system spots an error and provides advice in terms of the goals and plans that should solve the problem. |
| Effect: | improved learning of programming plans and procedures |
| Dependencies: | detection and diagnosis of user errors, plans, and procedures |
| Issues: | reactive learning, tutor initiative, contextual advice |
| Theory: | indirect theory grounding [Papert, 1980; Lewis & Anderson, 1985] |

# A.11   SELVIN'S QUESTMAP AND COMPENDIUM (1999)

**issue-based tools for capturing debates about wicked problems**

+ provide simple and straightforward ways to create and connect IBIS graphs

− lack the ability to scale to very large graphs

Selvin was inspired by the issue-based approaches to problem analysis, working with colleagues through the 1990s to develop a tool and process that would capture its power in an way that was accessible to a broad audience [Selvin, 1999]. His team developed Compendium (earlier known as QuestMap). The figure shown here, based on one generated in 1998 and appearing in Selvin [1999], shows how a question can be broken into sub-questions and ultimately into potential ideas for addressing the questions.

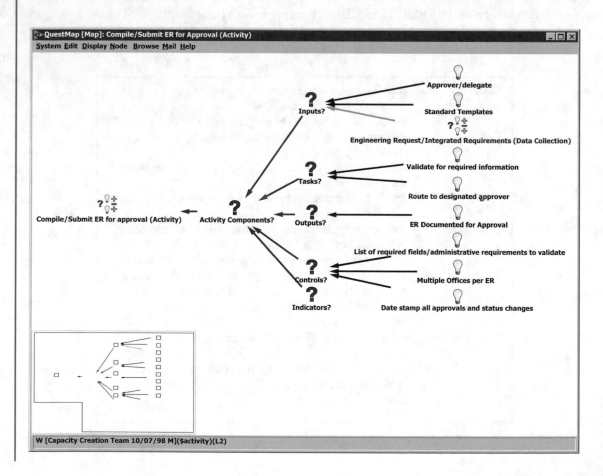

# A.12  CLAIMS IN THE ROSSON AND CARROLL TEXTBOOK (2002)

**the simplified claims targeted at an educational audience**

+ are highly accessible to students who are learning about approaches to HCI for the first time

− lack the quantity of knowledge found in other claims representations

Rosson and Carroll's 2002 textbook provided a view of scenario-based development of user interfaces that was tailored for students, using a simplified version of claims as a way to analyze scenarios. A running case study in the book explores a virtual science fair, with an evolving set of scenarios and claims as the case study progresses from requirements analysis to activity design to information and interaction design to evaluation. A claim from the interaction design part of the case study is given here [Rosson and Carroll, 2002, p. 187].

Viewing exhibit elements by selecting its miniature view
+ leverages experience with radio-button selection mechanisms
+simplifies a quick browse by "poking" one icon after another
- but requires viewers to alternate attention from main window to controls

## A.13   VAN DUYNE'S PATTERNS (2002)

**a collection of HCI patterns linked by color and shape**

+ provide easy-to-assimilate connections among patterns

− have limited scalability

van Duyne et al. [2002], 2006 created a highly visual example-rich book of interface design patterns, with color-coded sections and cross-references to support or provide alternatives for the pattern. Most patterns are multiple pages in length, and include a problem background and description, multiple solutions, and other patterns to consider. The example shot from the book shows a small portion of a pattern titled "Headlines and blurbs", seeking to address the need for "short descriptive headlines and blurbs to hook customers into clicking for more content". The book excerpt shows the color coded pages (shown at the right of the book excerpt), pointers to related and supporting claims (highlighted with the colored circles), and an example figure [van Duyne et al., 2002, p. 299].

**Put Headlines and Blurbs into Various Content Modules throughout the Site** •
To bring content to the fore, you must highlight it throughout the site, as headlines and as sidebars. Promote content pages using headlines and blurbs  in CONTENT MODULES (D2) on the HOMEPAGE PORTAL (C1) (see Figure D3.3), and in CONSISTENT SIDEBARS OF RELATED CONTENT (I6) (see Figure D3.4).

 If there are only a few headlines and blurbs, just use CHRONOLOGICAL ORGANIZATION (B6). A chronological structure makes it easier to find what's new, on the basis of the date.

**Figure D3.2**

A content file or record might show information in this way in a database.

```
ArticleNumber: 12345
Headline: For Whom Pacific Bell
Tolls
Blurb: Long derided for poor
customer service by its DSL
subscribers, Pacific Bell has
continued to over-commit on DSL
installations as it tries to beat
the cable industry in the broadband
Internet services business. So why
is Pacific Bell still a good
investment?
PubDate: 20010511
Author: Alexander Graham
Copyright: 2001 NewArch Media, Inc.
ContentHome: Utilities
```

# A.14  HAYNES' CLAIMS ANALYSIS (2004)

**aggregating knowledge in a claims library during an evaluation**

+ reflect the value of a claims-based analysis

+ can generate explanations for performance of hypothetical or implemented design

− can yield vague benefits that require additional exploration and evaluation

Haynes and his colleagues augmented the claims in a scenario-based evaluation to anchor the evaluation in real-world contexts [Haynes et al., 2004]. They found that their approach helped them to focus the evaluation and identify contributions, contextual factors, and opportunities for future work within a design space. In the paper, they aggregate claims into types according to their potential benefits (measurable, tangible, intangible) to understand the benefits and focus future evaluation.

| Claim Type | Frequency | % |
|---|---|---|
| Measurable Benefits | 11 6 | |
| Tangible Benefits | 54 | 26 |
| Intangible Benefits | 147 68 | |
| **Total Positive Claims** | **212** | **100** |

## A.15   CHEWAR'S CLAIMS AND CRITICAL PARAMETERS (2004)

**claims that include critical parameter values**

+ can be indexed, searched, grouped, and compared

− but add a level of complexity to claim creation and use

Chewar sought ways to formally assess a claims, with a focus on the domain of notification systems [Chewar, 2005]. She and her colleagues [Chewar et al., 2004b] introduced a critical parameter indexing scheme, whereby three critical parameter values are calculated for each claim based on assessed usability characteristics. In the example (from Chewar, 2005), while the textual descriptions are reasonably easy to read and understand, the critical parameter values (labeled with I, R, and C) support comparison across large sets of claims and promote easy understanding among designers.

| |
|---|
| Bulletin board metaphor with notifications as notes on a board<br>+ causes moderate user reaction<br>+ causes only mild interruption<br>+ promotes high comprehension<br><br>I: 0.35<br>R: 0.54<br>C: 0.62 |

| |
|---|
| Waterfall metaphor with notifications as slowly descending icons<br>+ promotes high comprehension<br>+ causes only mild interruption<br>- results in low user reaction<br><br>I: 0.37<br>R: 0.37<br>C: 0.66 |

# A.16  SAPONAS' PRE-PATTERNS (2006)

**early-stage pre-patterns**

+ encourage discovery, idea generation, and issue clarification

− may be of questionable quality

Patterns typically capture established design knowledge, though the 1998 CHI workshop (detailed earlier in this appendix) introduced *activity patterns* as a means to capture early knowledge to be used to inspire debate. Saponas and his colleagues revisited that theme in their *pre-patterns* work [Saponas et al., 2006], a term originally introduced in Chung et al. [2004]. Saponas leveraged the visual layout and key elements seen in prior work: name, group, image, synopsis, background, problem, solution(s), forces, evidence, and literature. The early nature of the solutions was meant to encourage discovery, idea generation, and issue clarification. The example here shows a detail for one pattern from the Saponas library.

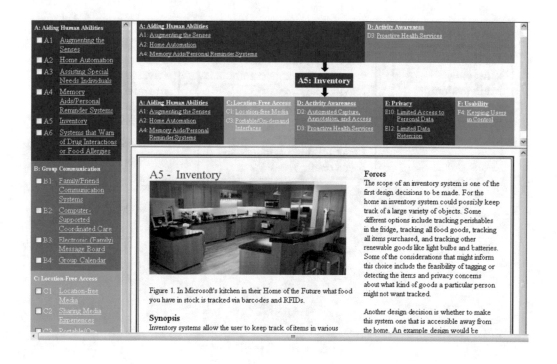

## A.17  LEE'S CLAIMS AND THE CENTRAL DESIGN RECORD (2009)

**the inclusion of claims as the central part of a goal-driven design and evaluation process**

+ provides an easy-to-generate knowledge unit that reflects positives and negatives to an approach to address a goal

+ highlights areas in need of prototyping or testing

— may be seen as excessive or unnecessary by developers

Lee et al. [2008] included claims as the central component of the Central Design Record (CDR), an agile method for connecting system design goals to usability testing needs. This example shows how a design claim evolved from an efficiency goal and was supported by a usability test (adopted from Lee et al., 2008).

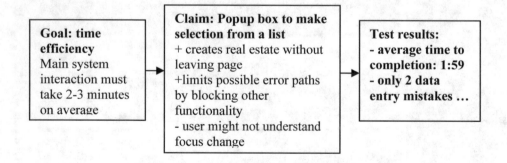

# A.18  INTUIO PATTERNS (2010)

**a domain-focused patterns library**

+ provides uniform data for patterns in the library to support domain-specific comparison and decision making

− may be difficult to determine which patterns belong in the library and which are external to the domain

Recent years have seen many large organizations like Yahoo! and IBM lead efforts in creating patterns languages, as well as smaller groups that often design patterns libraries for more focused domains. Web-based libraries can provide easier browsing and searching process that One particularly well-done library is Tom Zahler's HCI patterns for safety-related environments[5], that includes the usual patterns information like context, forces, and solution—but also interactive examples and the safety impact for many patterns from safety-critical environments [Zahler, 2010]. The interactive example here shows how a "combined input field" can provide immediate feedback through color change (to red) and a warning message (under the input box) when incorrect values are entered.

## Interactive Example

Call number / Client number

01 x    **Q**

Bitte eine gültige Rufnummer oder Lokations-ID eingeben.

---

[5]http://patterns.intuio.at

## A.19   WAHID'S CLAIM CARDS (2011)

**the use of images as an initial indicator about claim content**

\+ supports rapid high-level understanding about claim meaning

\− may lead to an incorrect assumption about the claims

Wahid looked for ways to make claims more accessible and easier to manipulate, exploring how a highly-visual card deck of claims could encourage people toward more creative design while still connecting them with the detailed rationale of a claim [Wahid et al., 2011]. Wahid and his colleagues created a set of cards, with one shown here, that presents a representative title and image (left) and a detailed claim (right). The cards were presented in both physical and virtual form to design teams to observe their use of the cards.

**Use of an information exhibit to notify users of public information**

\+ Takes advantage of group settings, making notifications to groups of users easier

\+ Typically can carry a higher density of information for notification

\- The information shown may not apply to all the users

\- May be harder to interact with a public information exhibit

*Add your own:*

# A.20 CULMSEE AND AWATI'S ISSUES AND COMPLEX PROBLEMS (2012)

**use of an issue-based tool like Compendium to support decision-making**

+ supports co-located synchronous assimilation of ideas

− limited support for distributed, asynchronous teams

− does not scale to large problems

Perhaps a sign that an approach has achieved wide impact is that someone *other* than the developers shows great proficiency in it—to the point that they write a book that features the approach. Culmsee and Awati [2011] authored a book titled *The Heretic's Guide to Best Practices: The Reality of Managing Complex Problems* that features wicked problems and issue-based approaches to them. The figure shown here, a detail from Awati's blog[6], shows an IBIS map created with Compendium that includes questions, ideas, pros and cons of ideas, questions that arise from one of the cons, and a decision.

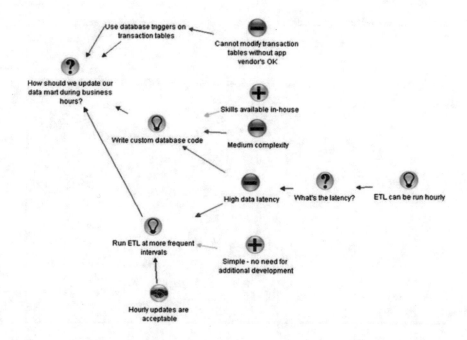

# Bibliography

Abraham, G. (2011) *Evaluating the Impact of a Pattern Structure on Communicating Interaction Design Advice*. Ph.D. Dissertation, Drexel University, Philadelphia, PA. Cited on page(s) 21

Abraham, G. and Atwood, M. E. (2009) Patterns or claims: Do they help in communicating design advice? In *Proceedings of the Australian Conference on Human-Computer Interaction (OZCHI 2009)*, 25–32. DOI: 10.1145/1738826.1738831 Cited on page(s) 21

Adams, M. J., Tenney, Y. K. and Pew, R. W. (1995) Situation awareness and the cognitive management of complex systems. *Human Factors* 37, 87–104. DOI: 10.1518/001872095779049462 Cited on page(s) 33

Alexander, C. (1979) *Timeless Way of Building*. Oxford: Oxford University Press. Cited on page(s) 19, 21

Alexander, C., Ishikawa, S., Silverstein, M., Jacobson, M., Fiksdahl-King, I. and Angel, S. (1977) *A Pattern Language*. Oxford: Oxford University Press. Cited on page(s) 19, 76

Amabile, T. M. (1982) Social psychology of creativity: A consensual assessment technique. *Journal of Personality and Social Psychology* 45(2), 357–376. DOI: 10.1037/0022-3514.45.2.357 Cited on page(s) 49

Bacon, F. (1605/1970). *Of the proficience and advancement of learning, divine and humane*. New York, NY: Da Cappo Press. Cited on page(s) 9

Bailey, B. P. and Iqbal, S. T. (2008) Understanding changes in mental workload during execution of goal-directed tasks and its application for interruption management. *ACM Transactions on Computer-Human Interaction* 14(4), 1–28. DOI: 10.1145/1314683.1314689 Cited on page(s) 32

Bayle, E., Bellamy, R., Casaday, G., Erickson, T., Fincher, S., Grinter, B., Gross, B., Lehder, D., Marmolin, H., Moore, B., Potts, C., Skousen, G. and Thomas, J. (1997) Putting it all together: Towards a pattern language for interaction design: A CHI 97 workshop. *SIGCHI Bulletin* 30(1). DOI: 10.1145/280571.280580 Cited on page(s) 20, 82

Begeman, M. L. and Conklin, J. (1988) The right tool for the job. *Byte Magazine*. Cited on page(s) 13, 77

Belady, L., and Richter, C. (1985) The MCC software technology program. *ACM SIGSOFT Software Engineering Notes* 10(3), 33–36. DOI: 10.1145/1012483.1012486 Cited on page(s) 13

Benyon, D. and Macaulay, C. (2002) Scenarios and the HCI-SE design problem. *Interacting with Computers* 14(2), 397–405. DOI: 10.1016/S0953-5438(02)00007-3 Cited on page(s) 27

Bhatia, S. and McCrickard, D. S. (2006) Listening to your inner voices: Investigating means for voice notifications. In *Proceedings of the ACM Conference on Human Factors in Computing Systems (CHI 2006)*, 1173–1176. DOI: 10.1145/1124772.1124947 Cited on page(s) xi, 43, 45

Birnholtz, J. P., Finholt, T. A., Horn, D. B., Bae., S. J. (2005). Grounding needs: Achieving common ground via lightweight chat in large, distributed, ad-hoc groups. In Proceedings of the ACM Conference on Human Factors in Computing Systems (CHI 2005), 21-30. Cited on page(s) 66

Boden, M. A. (1994) *Dimensions of Creativity*. Cambridge, MA: MIT Press. Cited on page(s) 49

Booth, W. C., Williams, J. M. and Colomb, G. G. (1995/2003/2008) *The Craft of Research*. Chicago, IL: The University of Chicago Press. Cited on page(s) 12

Borchers, J. (2001) *A Pattern Approach to Interaction Design*. New York: Wiley. Cited on page(s) 20, 21

Borchers, J. and Thomas, J. (2001) Patterns? What's in it for HCI? In *Extended Abstracts of the ACM Conference on Human Factors in Computing Systems (CHI 2001)*, 225–226. DOI: 10.1145/634067.634201 Cited on page(s) 20

Branham, S. M. (2009) Whatever Became of Claims? Boaster paper at the *Human Computer Interaction Consortium (HCIC) Annual Meeting*, Winter Park, CO. Cited on page(s) 13

Branham, S. M., Harrison, S. and McCrickard, D. S. (2010) Making design rationale matter: How design rationale has failed and how it can succeed again. Boaster paper at the *Human Computer Interaction Consortium (HCIC) Annual Meeting*, Winter Park, CO. Cited on page(s) 13

Buckingham Shum, S. (1996) Analyzing the usability of a design rationale notation. In Moran, T. P. and Carroll, J. M., Eds., *Design Rationale: Concepts, Techniques, and Use*, 185–215. Cited on page(s) 18

Buckingham Shum, S., Selvin, A., Sierhuis, M., Conklin, J., Haley, C. and Nuseibeh, B. (2006) Hypermedia support for argumentation-based rationale: 15 years on from gIBIS and QOC. In Dutoit, A., McCall, R., Mistrik, I. and Paech, B., Eds., *Rationale Management in Software Engineering*, 111–132. Cited on page(s) 15, 18

Burge, J. E. (2005) *Software Engineering Using RATionale*. Ph.D. Dissertation, Worcester Polytechnic Institute, Worcester, MA. Cited on page(s) 11

Burge, J. E. and Brown, D. C. (2012) SEURAT: Integrated rationale management. In *Proceedings of the International Conference on Software Engineering (ICSE)*, to appear. Cited on page(s) 69

Burge, J. E., Carroll, J. M., McCall, R. and Mistrik, I. (2008) *Rationale-Based Software Engineering.* Springer. DOI: 10.1007/978-3-540-77583-6 Cited on page(s) 27, 59

Bush, V. (1945) As we may think. *Atlantic Monthly* 176, 101–108. DOI: 10.1145/227181.227186 Cited on page(s) 10

Buxton, B. (2007) *Sketching User Experiences: Getting the Design Right and the Right Design.* San Francisco: Morgan Kaufman. Cited on page(s) 55, 56

Cadiz, J. J., Venolia, G., Jancke, G. and Gupta, A. (2002) Designing and deploying an information awareness interface. In *Proceedings of the ACM Conference on Computer Supported Cooperative Work (CSCW 2002)*, 314–323. DOI: 10.1145/587078.587122 Cited on page(s) 51

Carroll, J. M. (1997) Human-computer interaction: Psychology as a science of design. *International Journal of Human-Computer Studies* 46(2-3), 501–522. Cited on page(s) 25

Carroll, J. M. (2000). *Making Use: Scenario-Based Design of Human-Computer Interactions.* Cambridge, MA: MIT Press. Cited on page(s) 23, 26

Carroll, J. M. (2010) Conceptualizing a possible discipline of human-computer interaction. *Interacting with Computers* 22, 3–12. DOI: 10.1016/j.intcom.2009.11.008 Cited on page(s) 1, 2, 3, 6, 18

Carroll, J. M. (2011) Guest editor's introduction: Creativity and rationale in software design. *Human Technology* 7(2), 106–108. Cited on page(s) 6, 18, 30

Carroll, J. M. and Kellogg, W. K. (1989) Artifact as theory-nexus: Hermeneutics meets theory-based design. In *Proceedings of the ACM Conference on Human Factors in Computing Systems (CHI 1989)*, 7–14. DOI: 10.1145/67450.67452 Cited on page(s) 4, 7, 11, 23, 24, 28, 42, 78

Carroll, J. M., Mack, R. L., Robertson, S. P. and Rosson M. B. (1994) Binding objects to scenarios of use. *International Journal of Human-Computer Studies* 41, 243–276. DOI: 10.1006/ijhc.1994.1058 Cited on page(s) 24

Carroll, J. M. and Moran, T. P. (1991) Introduction to his special issue on design rationale. *Human-Computer Interaction* 6(3), 197–200. Cited on page(s) 24, 25

Carroll J. M. and Rosson, M. B. (1992) Getting around the task-artifact cycle: How to make claims and design by scenario. *ACM Transactions on Information Systems* 10(2), 181–212. DOI: 10.1145/146802.146834 Cited on page(s) 5, 9, 24, 80

Carroll, J. M., Singley, M. S. and Rosson, M. B. (1992) Integrating theory development with design evaluation. *Behaviour and Information Technology* 11, 247–255. DOI: 10.1080/01449299208924345 Cited on page(s) 24, 66

Chewar, C. M. (2005) *User-Centered Critical Parameters for Design Specification, Evaluation, and Reuse: Modeling Goals and Effects of Notification Systems.* Ph.D. Dissertation, Department of Computer Science, Virginia Tech, July 2005. Cited on page(s) 5, 6, 24, 25, 31, 36, 60, 88

Chewar, C. M., Bachetti, E., McCrickard, D. S. and Booker, J. E. (2004a) Automating a design reuse facility with critical parameters: Lessons learned in developing the LINK-UP system. In *Proceedings of the Conference on Computer-Aided Design of User Interfaces (CADUI)*, 236–247. DOI: 10.1007/1-4020-3304-4_19 Cited on page(s) 6

Chewar, C. M., McCrickard, D. S. and Sutcliffe, A. G. (2004b) Unpacking critical parameters for interface design: Evaluating systems with the IRC framework. In *Proceedings of the ACM Conference on Designing Interactive Systems (DIS)*, 279–288. DOI: 10.1145/1013115.1013155 Cited on page(s) xi, 6, 30, 31, 32, 36, 88

Chung, E., Hong., J. I., Lin, J., Prabaker, M. K., Landay, J. A. and Liu, A. (2004) Development and evaluation of emerging design patterns for ubiquitous computing. In *Proceedings of the ACM Conference on Designing Interactive Systems (DIS 2004)*, 233–242. DOI: 10.1145/1013115.1013148 Cited on page(s) 21, 89

Clark, H. H. (1992) *Arenas of Language Use.* Chicago, IL: The University of Chicago Press. Cited on page(s) 65

Clark, H. H. (1996) *Using Language.* Cambridge: Cambridge University Press. Cited on page(s) 65

Conklin, J. (2005) *Dialogue Mapping: Building Shared Understanding of Wicked Problems.* New York: Wiley. Cited on page(s) 15, 18, 51

Conklin, J., Selvin, A., Buckingham Shum, S. and Sierhuis, M. (2001) Facilitated hypertext for collective sensemaking: 15 years on from gIBIS. In *Proceedings of the 12th ACM Conference on Hypertext and Hypermedia*, 123–124. DOI: 10.1145/504216.504246 Cited on page(s) 18

Conklin, J. and Yakemovic, K. (1988) gIBIS: A hypertext tool for exploratory policy discussion. *ACM Transactions on Office Information Systems* 6(4), 303–331. DOI: 10.1145/58566.59297 Cited on page(s) 13

Conklin, J. and Yakemovic, K. (1991) A process-oriented approach to design rationale. *Human-Computer Interaction* 6(3/4), 357–391. DOI: 10.1207/s15327051hci0603&4_6 Cited on page(s) 13

Consiglio, T. and van der Veer, G. (2011) Designing an interactive learning environment for a world-wide distance adult learning community. In *Proceedings of the 29th Annual European Conference on Cognitive Ergonomics (ECCE (2011)*, 225–228. DOI: 10.1145/2074712.2074758 Cited on page(s) 21

Cooper, A. (1999) *The Inmates are Running the Asylum*. New York, NY: Macmillan. Cited on page(s) 27

Cooper, A. and Reimann, R. (2003) *About Face 2.0: The Essentials of Interaction*. New York: Wiley. Cited on page(s) 19, 27

Cooper, A., Reimann, R. and Cronin, D. (2007) *About Face 3: The Essentials of Interaction Design*. New York: Wiley. Cited on page(s) 27

Culmsee, P. (2012) Personal communication (via blog post response). Available at `http://mccricks.wordpress.com/2011/10/07/compendium-review/` Cited on page(s) 15

Culmsee, P. and Awati, K. (2011) *The Heretic's Guide to Best Practices*. The Reality of Managing Complex Problems in Organisations. Cited on page(s) 15, 51, 93

Cutrell, E., Czerwinski, M. and Horvitz, E (2001) Notification, disruption, and memory: Effects of messaging interruptions on memory and performance. In *Proceedings of the IFIP TC. 13 International Conference on Human-Computer Interaction (INTERACT 2001)*, 263–269. Cited on page(s) 32

Dearden, A. and Finlay, J. (2006) Pattern languages in HCI: A critical review. *Human Computer Interaction* 21(1), 49–102. DOI: 10.1207/s15327051hci2101_3 Cited on page(s) 21, 59

Diaper, D. (2002) Scenarios and task analysis. *Interacting with Computers* 14, 379–395. DOI: 10.1016/S0953-5438(02)00005-X Cited on page(s) 1, 27

Dourish, P. (2001). *Where The Action Is: The Foundations of Embodied Interaction*. Cambridge, MA: MIT Press. Cited on page(s) 3

Dutoit, A. H., McCall, R., Mistrik I. and Paech, B. (Eds.) (2006) *Rationale Management in Software Engineering*. Berlin: Springer. DOI: 10.1007/978-3-540-30998-7 Cited on page(s) 14, 18

Endsley, M. R., Bolte, B. and Jones, D. G. (2003) *Designing for Situation Awareness: An Approach to User-Centered Design*. New York: Taylor and Francis. Cited on page(s) 33

Fabian, A., Felton, D., Grant, M., Montabert, C., Pious, K., Rashidi, N., Tarpley III, A. R., Taylor, N., Chewar, C. M., and McCrickard, D. S. (2004). Designing the claims reuse library: Validating classification methods for notification systems. In *Proceedings of the ACM Southeast Conference (ACMSE 2004)*, 357-362. Cited on page(s) 5

Fallman, D. (2003). Design-oriented human-computer interaction. In Proceedings of the ACM Conference on Human Factors in Computing Systems (CHI 2003), 225-232. Cited on page(s) 2

Finch, C. (1973) *The Art of Walt Disney: From Mickey Mouse to the Magic Kingdom*. New York: Harry Abrams. Cited on page(s) 55

Fincher, S., Finlay, J., Greene, S, Jones, L., Matchen, P., Thomas, J. and Molina, P. J. (2003) Perspectives on HCI patterns: Concepts and tools. In *Conference Companion of the Conference on Human Factors in Computing Systems (CHI 2003)*, 1044–1045. DOI: 10.1145/765891.766140 Cited on page(s) 20

Fischer, G., McCall, R. and Morch, A. (1989) Design environments for constructive and argumentative design. In *Proceedings of the ACM Conference on Human Factors in Computing Systems (CHI 1989)*, 269–275. DOI: 10.1145/67450.67501 Cited on page(s) 14

Flyvbjerg, B. (2001) *Making Social Science Matter: Why Social Inquiry Fails and How It Can Succeed Again*. Cambridge University Press. Cited on page(s) 9

Fox, D., Sillito, J. and Maurer, F. (2008) Agile methods and user-centered design: How these two methodologies are being successfully integrated in industry. In *Proceedings of the 2008 Agile Conference (Agile 2008)*, 63–72. DOI: 10.1109/Agile.2008.78 Cited on page(s) 38, 39

Gamma, E., Helm, R., Johnson, R., and Vlissides, J. (1995). *Design Patterns: Elements of Reusable Object-Oriented Software*. Addison-Wesley. Cited on page(s) 19, 81

Gaver, W. W. and Martin, H. (2000) Alternatives: Exploring information appliances through conceptual design proposals. In *Proceedings of the ACM Conference on Human Factors in Computing Systems (CHI 2000)*, 209–216. DOI: 10.1145/332040.332433 Cited on page(s) 2, 28, 30

Gaver, W. W., Smith, R. and O'Shea, T. (1991) Effective sounds in complex systems: The ARKola simulation. In *Proceedings of the ACM Conference on Human Factors in Computing Systems (CHI 1991)*, 85–90. DOI: 10.1145/108844.108857 Cited on page(s) 43

Gold, R. (2007) *The Plenitude: Creativity, Innovation, and Making Stuff*. Cambridge, MA: MIT Press. Cited on page(s) 29

Gray, W. D. and Salzman, M. C. (1998a). Damaged merchandise? A review of experiments that compare usability methods. *Human Computer Interaction 13* (3), 203-261. Cited on page(s) 3

Gray, W. D. and Salzman, M. C. (1998b). Repairing damaged merchandise: A rejoinder. *Human Computer Interaction 13* (3), 325-335. Cited on page(s) 3

Green, D. M. and Swetz, J. A. (1966) *Signal Detection Theory and Psychophysics*. New York: Wiley. Cited on page(s) 33

Grudin, J. (2005). Three Faces of Human-Computer Interaction. *IEEE Annals of the History of Computing 27*(4), 46-62. Cited on page(s) 2, 3, 29

Grudin, J. and Pruitt, J. (2002) Personas: Practice and theory. In *Proceedings of the 2003 Conference on Designing for User Experiences (DUX 2003)*, 1–15. DOI: 10.1145/997078.997089 Cited on page(s) 27

Guilford, J. (1950) Creativity. *American Psychologist* 5, 444–454. DOI: 10.1037/h0063487 Cited on page(s) 49

Halasz, F. (1988) Reflections on notecards: Seven issues for the next generation of hypertext systems. *Communications of the ACM* 31(7), 836–852. DOI: 10.1145/48511.48514 Cited on page(s) 18

Halverson, C. (1994) Distributed cognition as a theoretical framework for HCI: Don't throw the baby out with the bathwater—the importance of the cursor in air traffic control. Technical report 9403, Department of Cognitive Science, University of California San Diego, San Diego, CA. Cited on page(s) 65, 66

Harrison, B. L., Ishii, H., Vicente, K. J. and Buxton, W. A. (1995) Transparent layered user interfaces: An evaluation of a display design to enhance focused and divided attention. In *Proceedings of the ACM Conference on Human Factors in Computing Systems (CHI 1995)*, 317–324. DOI: 10.1145/223904.223945 Cited on page(s) 65

Harrison, S., Tatar, D., and Sengers, P. (2007). The three paradigms of HCI. In *alt.chi Proceedings of the ACM Conference on Human Factors in Computing Systems (CHI 2007)*. Cited on page(s) 2, 3, 29

Hart, J. (1999) *The Art of the Storyboard: Storyboarding for Film, TV, and Animation*. Amsterdam: Focal Press. Cited on page(s) 55

Haynes, S. R., Purao, S. and Skattebo, A. L. (2004) Situating evaluation in scenarios of use. In *Proceedings of the ACM Conference on Computer Supported Cooperative Work (CSCW 2004)*, 92–101. DOI: 10.1145/1031607.1031624 Cited on page(s) 27, 87

Hennipman, E.-J., Oppelaar, E.-J. and van der Veer, G. (2008) Pattern languages as tool for discount usability engineering. In Nicholas Graham, T.C. and Palanque, P., Eds., *Interactive Systems: Design, Specification, and Verification*, 108–120, Heidelberg: Springer. DOI: 10.1007/978-3-540-70569-7_11 Cited on page(s) 21

Herring, S. R., Chang, C. C., Krantzler, J. and Bailey, B. P. (2009) Getting inspired! Understanding how and why examples are used in creative design practice. In *Proceedings of the ACM Conference on Human Factors in Computing Systems (CHI 2009)*, 87–96. DOI: 10.1145/1518701.1518717 Cited on page(s) 55

Horvitz, E. and Apacible, J. (2003) Learning and reasoning about interruption. In *Proceedings of the Fifth International Conference on Multimodal Interfaces (ICMI)*, 20–27. DOI: 10.1145/958432.958440 Cited on page(s) 32, 34

Hutchins, E. (1995) *Cognition in the Wild*. Cambridge, MA: MIT Press. Cited on page(s) 65, 66

IDEO Method Cards. (2003). Available from `ideo.com/work/method-cards`. Cited on page(s) 70

Johnson, W. L. (1985) *Intention-Based Diagnosis of Errors in Novice Programs*. Ph.D. Dissertation, Yale University, New Haven, CT. Cited on page(s) 83

Karam, M., Lee, J. C., Rose, T., Quek, F. and McCrickard, D. S. (2009) Comparing gesture and touch for notification system interaction. In *Proceedings of the 2009 IARIA Conference on Advances in Computer Human Interaction (ACHI)*, 7–12. DOI: 10.1109/ACHI.2009.65 Cited on page(s) xi, 43, 45, 47, 48

Kellaher, K. (1999) *101 Picture Prompts to Spark Super Writing: Photographs, Cartoons, Art Masterpieces to Intrigue, Amuse, Inspire Every Writer in Your Class*. New York: Scholastic Professional Books. Cited on page(s) 54

Kunz, W. and Rittel, H. W. J. (1970) Issues as elements of information systems. Working paper number 131, Studiengruppe für Systemforschung, Heidelberg, Germany. Cited on page(s) 13, 17, 75

Lafreniere, D., and Hedenskog, A. (2001). Describing and using patterns for UI design. In *Extended Proceedings of the Usability Professionals Association Annual Conference*. Cited on page(s) 21

Larsson, A., Warell, A., Magnusson, C. and Eftring, H. (2011) Dynamic User Experiences: Context is Everything. Workshop proceedings, available from haptimap.org Cited on page(s) 55, 70

Lee, J. (1991) Extending the Potts and Bruns model for recording design rationale. In *Proceedings of the 10th International Conference on Software Engineering (ICSE 1988)*, 418–427. DOI: 10.1109/ICSE.1991.130629 Cited on page(s) 14

Lee, J. C., Judge, T. K. and McCrickard, D. S. (2011) Evaluating eXtreme scenario-based design in a distributed team. In *Conference Companion of the 2011 ACM Conference on Human Factors in Computing Systems (CHI 2011)*, 863–877. DOI: 10.1145/1979742.1979681 Cited on page(s) xi, 30, 37, 39, 42

Lee, J. C. and McCrickard, D. S. (2007) Toward extreme(ly) usably software: Exploring tensions between usability and agile software development. In *Proceedings of the 2007 Conference on Agile Software Development (Agile 2007)*, 59–71. DOI: 10.1109/AGILE.2007.63 Cited on page(s) 37, 39

Lee, J. C., McCrickard, D. S. and Stevens, K. T. (2008) Examining the foundations of agile usability with eXtreme scenario-based design. In *Proceedings of the 2009 Conference on Agile Software Development (Agile 2009)*, 3–10. DOI: 10.1109/AGILE.2009.30 Cited on page(s) xi, 37, 38, 39, 42, 90

Long, J. and Dowell, J. (1989) Conceptions of the discipline of HCI: Craft, applied science, and engineering. In *People and Computers V: Proceedings of the Fifth Conference of the British Computer Society*, 9–32. DOI: 10.2277/0521384303 Cited on page(s) 1, 29

Luyten, K., Vanacken, D., Weiss, M., Borchers, J., Izadi, S., and Wigdor, D. (2011). Engineering patterns for multi-touch interfaces. In *Proceedings of the 2$^{nd}$ ACM SIGCHI Symposium on Engineering Interactive Computing Systems (EICS)*, 365-366. Cited on page(s) 20, 21

Luyten, K., Vanacken, D., Weiss, M., Borchers, J., Nacenta, M. (2011). Second Workshop on Engineering Patterns for Multi-touch Interfaces. In *Proceedings of the 3$^{rd}$ ACM SIGCHI Symposium on Engineering Interactive Computing Systems (EICS)*, 335-336. Cited on page(s) 20, 21

Maclean, A., Young, R. M., Bellotti, V. M. E. and Moran, T. (1996) Questions, options, and criteria: Elements of design space analysis. In Moran, T. P. and Carroll, J. M., Eds., *Design Rationale Concepts, Techniques and Use*, 53–106. Cited on page(s) 14

McCall, R. (1989) MIKROPLIS: A hypertext system for design. *Design Studies* 10(4), 228–238. DOI: 10.1016/0142-694X(89)90006-9 Cited on page(s) 13, 14

McCall, R., Bennett, P. and d'Oronzio, P. (1990) PHIDIAS: A PHI-based design environment integrating CAD graphics into dynamic hypertext. In *Proceedings of the 1990 European Conference on Hypertext (ECHT '90)*, 152–165. Cited on page(s) 14

McCall, R. J. (1991) PHI: A conceptual foundation for design hypermedia. *Design Studies* 12(1), 30–41. DOI: 10.1016/0142-694X(91)90006-I Cited on page(s) 13, 14, 79

McCall, R. J. (2012) Personal communication. DOI: 10.1007/BF02633361 Cited on page(s) 69

McCall, R. J., Bennett, P. R., D'Oronzio, P. S., Oswald, J. L., Shipman, F. M. and Wallace, N. F. (1992) PHIDIAS: Integrating CAD graphics into dynamic hypertext. In *Hypertext: Concepts, Systems, and Applications*. Cambridge: Cambridge University Press, 152–165. Cited on page(s) 14

McCrickard, D. S., Atwood, M. E., Curtis, G., Harrison, S., Kolko, J., Stolterman, E. and Wahid, S. (2010) Artifacts in design: Representation, ideation, and process. In *Conference Companion to the ACM Conference on Human Factors in Computing Systems (CHI 2010)*, 4445–4448. DOI: 10.1145/1753846.1754170 Cited on page(s) 30, 70

McCrickard, D. S., Catrambone, R., Chewar, C. M., and Stasko, J. (2003a) Establishing tradeoffs that leverage attention for utility: Empirically evaluating information display in notification systems. DOI: 10.1016/S1071-5819(03)00022-3 Cited on page(s) 4, 32

McCrickard, D. S., Chewar, C. M., Somervell, J. P. and Ndiwalana, A. (2003b) A model for notification systems evaluation—Assessing user goals for multitasking activity. *Transactions on Computer Human Interaction* 10(4), 312–338. DOI: 10.1145/966930.966933 Cited on page(s) 31, 35, 46, 56

McCrickard, D. S., Czerwinski, M. and Bartram, L. (2003c) Introduction: design and evaluation of notification user interfaces. *Int. J. Hum.-Comput. Stud.* 58(5), 509–514. DOI: 10.1016/S1071-5819(03)00025-9 Cited on page(s) 32

McCrickard, D. S. and Chewar, C. M. (2003). Attuning notification design to user goals and attention costs. Communications of the ACM 46 (3), 67-72. Cited on page(s) 34

McCrickard, D. S., Chewar, C. M. and Somervell, J. P. (2004) Design, science, and engineering topics? Teaching HCI with a unified method. In *Proceedings of the ACM Technical Symposium on Computer Science Education (SIGCSE 2004)*, 31–35. DOI: 10.1145/971300.971314 Cited on page(s) xi, 29

McCrickard, D. S., Wahid, S., Branham, S. M. and Harrison, S. (2011) Achieving both creativity and rationale: Reuse in design with images and claims. *Human Technology* 7(2), 109–122. Cited on page(s) xii, 49, 54, 55

McFarlane, D. C. (2002) Comparison of four primary methods for coordinating the interruption of people in human-computer interaction. *Human-Computer Interaction* 17(3), 63-139. DOI: 10.1207/S15327051HCI1701_2 Cited on page(s) 32

Michalko, M. (2006) *Thinkertoys*. Berkeley, CA: Ten Speed Press. Cited on page(s) 54

Moran, T. P. and Carroll, J. M. (Eds.) (1996) *Design Rationale: Concepts, Techniques, and Use*. Mahwah, NJ: Lawrence Erlbaum Associates. Cited on page(s) 3, 18, 24, 25

Nass, C. and Gong, L. (2000) Speech interfaces from an evolutionary perspective. *Communications of the ACM* 43(9), 36–43. DOI: 10.1145/348941.348976 Cited on page(s) 43

Nathan, L., Friedman, B. and Hendry, D. (2009) Sustainably ours: Information system design as catalyst: Human action and environmental sustainability. *Interactions* 16(4), 6–11. DOI: 10.1145/1551986.1551988 Cited on page(s) 55

Newman, W. M. (1997) Better or just different? On the benefits of designing interactive systems in terms of critical parameters. In *Proceedings of the ACM Conference on Designing Interactive Systems (DIS 1997)*, 239–245. DOI: 10.1145/263552.263615 Cited on page(s) 30

Newman, W. M., Taylor, A. S., Dance, C. R. and Taylor, S. A. (2000) Performance targets, models and innovation in interactive systems design. In *Proceedings of the ACM Conference on Designing Interactive Systems (DIS 2000)*, 381–387. DOI: 10.1145/347642.347796 Cited on page(s) 31

Norman, D. A. (1986) Cognitive Engineering. In Norman, D. A. and Draper, S. W., Eds., *User Centered Design: New Perspectives on Human Computer Interaction*, 31–62. Mahwah, NJ: Lawrence Erlbaum Associates. Cited on page(s) 31, 38, 50

Olson, G. M. and Moran, T. P. (1998). Commentary on "Damaged Merchandise?" *Human Computer Interaction 13* (3), 263-323. Cited on page(s) 3

Paternò, F. (2002) Discussion: Commentary on 'scenarios and task analysis' by Dan Diaper. *Interacting with Computers* 14(4), 407–409. DOI: 10.1016/S0953-5438(02)00008-5 Cited on page(s) 27

Patton, J. (2002) Hitting the target: Adding interaction design to agile software development. In *Proceedings of OOPSLA 2002*, 1–ff. DOI: 10.1145/604251.604255 Cited on page(s) 37

Payne, C., Allgood, C. F., Chewar, C. M., Holbrook, C. and McCrickard, D. S. (2003) Generalizing interface design knowledge: Lessons learned from developing a claims library. In *Proceedings of the 2003 IEEE International Conference on Information Reuse and Integration (IRI 2003)*, 362–369. Cited on page(s) 64

Potts, C. and Bruns, G. (1988) Recording the reasons for design decisions. In *Proceedings of the 10th International Conference on Software Engineering (ICSE 1988)*, 418–427. DOI: 10.1109/ICSE.1988.93722 Cited on page(s) 14

Pries-Heje, J. and Baskerville, R. (2008). The design theory nexus. *MIS Quarterly 32* (4), 731-755. Cited on page(s) 9

Rayward, W. B. (2003) Knowledge organisation and a new world polity: The rise and fall and rise of the ideas of Paul Otlet. *Transnational Associations* 1/2, 4–15. Cited on page(s) 11

Rittel, H. W. J. and Webber, M. (1973) Dilemmas in a general theory of planning. *Policy Sciences* 4, 155–169. DOI: 10.1007/BF01405730 Cited on page(s) 13, 18

Rosson, M. B. and Carroll, J. M. (2002) *Usability Engineering: Scenario-Based Development of Human-Computer Interaction*. London: Academic Press. Cited on page(s) 5, 23, 24, 26, 30, 36, 38, 50, 56, 64, 65, 85

Saponas, T. S., Prabaker, M. K., Abowd, G. D. and Landay, J. A. (2006) The impact of pre-patterns on the design of digital home applications. In *Proceedings of the ACM Conference on Designing Interactive Systems (DIS 2006)*, 189–198. DOI: 10.1145/1142405.1142436 Cited on page(s) 21, 60, 89

Sawhney, N. and Schmandt, C. (1999) Nomadic radio: Scaleable and contextual notification for wearable audio messaging. In *Proceedings of the ACM Conference on Human Factors in Computing Systems (CHI 1999)*, 96–103. DOI: 10.1145/302979.303005 Cited on page(s) 43

Schön, D. A. (1983). *The Reflective Practitioner: How Professionals Think in Action*. Temple Smith. Cited on page(s) 9

Schuler, W. and Smith, J. (1990) Authors argumentation assistant (AAA): A hypertext-based authoring tool for argumentative texts. In *Proceedings of the 1990 European Conference on Hypertext (ECHT '90)*, 137–151. Cited on page(s) 14

Schummer, T., Borchers, J., Thomas, J. C. and Zdun, U. (2004) Human-computer human-interaction patterns: Workshop on the human role in HCI patterns. In *Conference Companion of the Conference on Human Factors in Computing Systems (CHI 2004)*, 1721–1722. DOI: 10.1145/985921.986200 Cited on page(s) 20, 21

Selvin, A. (1999) Supporting collaborative analysis and design with hypertext functionality. *Journal of Digital Information* 1(4). Cited on page(s) 18, 84

Selvin, A. M. (2011) *Making Representations Matter: Understanding Practitioner Experience in Participatory Sensemaking.* Ph.D. Dissertation, The Open University. Cited on page(s) 18

Selvin, A. M., Buckingham Shum, S. J., Aakhus, M. (2010). The practice level in participatory design rationale: Studying practitioner moves and choices. *Human Technology* 6 (1), 71-105. Cited on page(s) 15

Sharp, H., Rogers, Y. and Preece, J. (2007) *Interaction Design: Beyond Human-Computer Interaction.* New York: John Wiley & Sons. Cited on page(s) 55

Simon, H.A. (1996). *The Sciences of the Artificial* ($3^{rd}$ edition). Cambridge, MA: MIT Press. Cited on page(s) 9

Singley, M. K. and Carroll, J. M. (1996) Synthesis by analysis: Five modes of reasoning that guide design. In Moran, T. P. and Carroll, J. M., Eds., *Design Rationale: Concepts, Techniques, and Use,* 241–265. Mahwah, NJ: Lawrence Erlbaum Associates. Cited on page(s) 50

Sutcliffe, A. G. (2006). Grand challenges in HCI: The quest for theory-led design. In *Proceedings of the HCI 2005 Conference on People and Computers XIX*, 491-505. Cited on page(s) 5, 27

Sutcliffe, A. G. (2010). Juxtaposing design representations for creativity. *Human Technology* 6 (1), 38-54. Cited on page(s) 5

Sutcliffe, A. S. (2000) On the effective use and reuse of HCI knowledge. *Transactions on Computer-Human Interaction* 7(2), 197–221. DOI: 10.1145/353485.353488 Cited on page(s) 25, 60

Sutcliffe, A. S. (2002) *The Domain Theory: Patterns for Knowledge and Software Reuse.* Mahwah, NJ: Lawrence Erlbaum Associates. Cited on page(s) 2, 6, 11, 23, 24, 26, 30, 59, 64, 83

Sutcliffe, A. S. and Carroll, J. M. (1999) Designing claims for reuse in interactive systems design. *International Journal of Human-Computer Studies* 50, 213–241. DOI: 10.1006/ijhc.1999.0245 Cited on page(s) 5, 25, 26, 50, 83

Tessendorf, D., Chewar, C. M., Ndiwalana, A., Pryor, J., McCrickard, D. S. and North, C. (2002) An ordering of secondary task display attributes. In *Extended Abstracts of the ACM Conference on Human Factors in Computing Systems (CHI 2002)*, 600–601. DOI: 10.1145/506443.506503 Cited on page(s) 32

Thomas, J. C. (2011). Focus on ego as universe and everyday sustainability. In *CHI Workshop on Everyday Practice and Sustainable HCI.* Cited on page(s) 21

Thomas, J. C. (2012) Understanding and harnessing conflict. In *CHI Workshop on Peace.* Cited on page(s) 21

Tidwell, J. (1998) Interaction patterns. In *Proceedings of the 1998 Conference on Patterns Languages of Programs (PLoP 1998)*. Cited on page(s) 20

Tidwell, J. (2005/2010) *Designing Interfaces*. Sebastopol, CA: O'Reilly. Cited on page(s) 21, 64

Toulmin, S. (1992) *Cosmopolis: The Hidden Agenda of Modernity*. New York, NY: Macmillan. Cited on page(s) 18

Toulmin, S. E. (1958/2003) *The Uses of Argument*. Cambridge: Cambridge University Press. Cited on page(s) 1, 11, 12, 23, 42, 74

Toulmin, S., Reike, R. and Janik, A. (1979) *An Introduction to Reasoning*. New York, NY: Macmillan. Cited on page(s) 12

Truong, K. N., Hayes, G. R. and Abowd, G. D. (2006) Storyboarding: An empirical determination of best practices and effective guidelines. In *Proceedings of the ACM Conference on Designing Interactive Systems (DIS 2006)*, 12–21. DOI: 10.1145/1142405.1142410 Cited on page(s) 55

van Dantzich, M., Robbins, D., Horvitz, E. and Czerwinski, M. (2002) Scope: Providing awareness of multiple notifications at a glance. In *Proceedings of the 6th International Working Conference on Advanced Visual Interfaces (AVI 2002)*, 267–281. DOI: 10.1145/1556262.1556306 Cited on page(s) 34

van den Heuvel, C. and Rayward, W. B. (2011) Facing interfaces: Paul Otlet's visualizations of data integration. *Journal of the American Society for Information Science and Technology* 62(12), 2313–2326. DOI: 10.1002/asi.21607 Cited on page(s) 11

van Duyne, D. K., Landay, J. A. and Hong, J. I. (2002/2006) *The Design of Sites: Patterns for Creating Winning Web Sites*. Englewood Cliffs, NJ: Prentice Hall. Cited on page(s) 21, 60, 86

van Setten, M., van der Veer, G. C., and Brinkkemper, S. (1997). Comparing interaction design techniques: A method for objective comparison to find the conceptual basis for interaction design. In *Proceedings of the ACM Conference on Designing Interactive Systems (DIS 1997)*, 349-357. Cited on page(s) 2

von Oech, R. (2008) *A Whack on the Side of the Head*. New York: Hachette Book Group. Cited on page(s) 54, 70

Wahid, S., Allgood, C. F., Chewar, C. M. and McCrickard, D. S. (2004) Entering the heart of design: Relationships for tracing claim evolution. In *Proceedings of the 16th International Conference on Software Engineering and Knowledge Engineering (SEKE 2004)*, 167–172. Cited on page(s) 6, 63, 64

Wahid, S., Branham, S. M., Cairco, L., McCrickard, D. S. and Harrison, S. (2009) Picking up arti-
facts: Storyboarding as a gateway to reuse. In *Proceedings of the IFIP TC. 13 Conference on Human-
Computer Interaction (INTERACT 2009)*, 528–541. DOI: 10.1007/978-3-642-03658-3_57
Cited on page(s) xii, 6, 30, 49, 54

Wahid, S., Branham, S. M., McCrickard, D. S. and Harrison, S. (2010) Investigating the relationship
between imagery and rationale in design. In *Proceedings of the 2010 ACM Conference on Designing
Interactive Systems (DIS 2010)*, 75–84. DOI: 10.1145/1858171.1858187  Cited on page(s) xii, 5,
49, 54, 70

Wahid, S. and McCrickard, D. S. (2006) Claims maps: Treasure maps for scenario-based design.
In *Proceedings of the World Conference on Educational Multimedia/Hypermedia and Educational
Telecommunications (ED-MEDIA 2006)*, 553–560. Cited on page(s) 50, 64

Wahid, S., McCrickard, D. S., DeGol, J., Elias, N. and Harrison, S. (2011) Don't drop it! Pick it up
and storyboard. In *Proceedings of the 2011 ACM Conference on Human Factors in Computing Systems
(CHI 2011)*, 1571–1580. DOI: 10.1145/1978942.1979171  Cited on page(s) xii, 5, 49, 54, 70, 92

Wahid, S. S. (2011) *Facilitating Design Knowledge Reuse through Relationships*. Ph.D. Dissertation,
Department of Computer Science, Virginia Tech, Blacksburg, VA. Cited on page(s) 6, 25, 51

Wania, C. (2008) *Examining the Impact of an Information Retrieval Pattern Language on the Design
of Information Retrieval Interfaces*. Ph.D. Dissertation, Drexel University, Philadelphia, PA. Cited
on page(s) 19, 21, 59

Whittaker, S., Terveen, L. and Nardi, B. A. (2000) Let's stop pushing the envelope and start addressing it: A reference task agenda for HCI. *Human-Computer Interaction* 15, 75–106.
DOI: 10.1207/S15327051HCI1523_2 Cited on page(s) 31, 33

Wickens, C. D. and Hollands, J. G. (1999) *Engineering Psychology and Human Performance*, 3rd ed.,
Englewood Cliffs, NJ: Prentice Hall. Cited on page(s) 32

Wright, A. (2007) *Glut: Mastering Information through the Ages*. Ithaca, NY: Cornell University Press.
Cited on page(s) 10

Zahler, T. (2010) *A Usability Engineering Lifecycle for Applications in Safety-Related Environments*.
Ph.D. Dissertation, University of Technology Vienna, Vienna, Austria. Cited on page(s) 91

# Author's Biography

## D. SCOTT MCCRICKARD

**D. Scott McCrickard** is an Associate Professor in the Department of Computer Science at Virginia Tech, and a member of Virginia Tech's Center for Human Computer Interaction. His research is on the design of mobile interfaces and notification systems, toward understanding how designers capture, share, and reuse design knowledge. He has received best paper awards from the Internet Research Journal, the IFIP Interact Conference, and the Advances in Computer-Human Interactions Conference. In 1992, he received an undergraduate degree in mathematical science from the University of North Carolina, Chapel Hill. He went on to receive his M.S. and Ph.D. degrees from Georgia Tech in computer science in 1995 and 2000, respectively. His sabbatical for the 2011–2012 academic year was at the University of Colorado, Boulder, where he authored this book.

Printed in the United States
by Baker & Taylor Publisher Services